DUCT TAPE
AND
DETERMINATION

DUCT TAPE AND DETERMINATION

A True Story of Turning Devastation into Grit

JACKY HUNT-BROERSMA

WITH CINDY KUZMA

FOREWORD BY MIRNA VALERIO

sourcebooks

Cover design by Emily Mahar
Front cover author photo provided by Jacky Hunt-Broersma
Cover images © nathamag11/Getty Images
Internal design by Tara Jaggers/Sourcebooks
Internal photos © Jacky Hunt-Broersma
Internal tape image © Kwangmoozaa/Getty Images

Published by Sourcebooks
1935 Brookdale RD, Naperville, IL 60563-2773
(630) 961-3900
sourcebooks.com

Cataloging-in-Publication Data is on file with the Library of Congress.

Printed and bound in the United States of America.
MA 10 9 8 7 6 5 4 3 2 1

To my incredible family, whose love and support made this book possible.

Foreword

Mirna Valerio

About one minute into a short video of me shot and produced by the folks at Garmin for their Women of Adventure series appears a beautiful brunette woman with two braids and a light blue tank top, wearing a hydration vest, ready to run. The year is 2019. The place, Buena Vista, Colorado, at the beginning of TransRockies three-day race, a prestigious ultramarathon that features 10,000 feet of vertical gain and around sixty miles of technical trail in the Colorado Rockies.

I had just met Jacky Hunt-Broersma in real life for the first time the previous day after having had a long, joyous conversation with her months before.

Hyland's, a natural homeopathy brand best known for its leg cramps ointment (and also one of my many very cool sponsors that year), was offering a sponsored spot in the race for one runner who demonstrated an extraordinary level of grit, perseverance, and optimism—all important qualities when contemplating running a challenging ultramarathon! Applications poured in from impressive and deserving runners, and I was honored to be part of the selection committee who got to conduct interviews with several of the applicants.

We offered the sponsored bib to Jacky, whose application spoke to us in ways that no others had. Because of a sudden health catastrophe, Jacky had been forced to change her life in unforeseeable ways. In her application we saw determination, pure athleticism, gratitude, and joy through her words and actions. I felt her giddiness through my cell phone when I got to share the news that she had been chosen as our contest winner. I couldn't wait to meet her and hug her in person a few months later.

I, like Jacky, am someone who folks tend to be somewhat curious about when they see me at races. Perhaps she and I are a kind of runner that people don't always get to see and experience frequently, so they may have some preconceived notions or assumptions about who we are and what we can do by virtue of how our human forms present. But enough of that! Times, they are a-changing. Runners of all shapes, ages, colors, sizes, and abilities are showing up to the start line, and this is exactly how we endeavor to help the world have a greater perspective and understanding of all bodies, which are all good bodies with intrinsic value and beauty.

In this inspirational and heartfelt memoir, you will find this beauty, with its attendant struggle and hardship. Through Jacky's eyes we see, as she writes so succinctly about the saguaro cacti in the desert at Javelina 100K, "models of endurance, adaptation, and resilience." This is who she is. After having her life turned upside down, she learns to give herself space, time, and grace to grieve and mourn, and then like the badass she is, pivots in a different direction and adapts to this new journey of necessity as a part of life's ever-changing, serpentine wiles. This is a lesson for all of us.

Life is complex, difficult, and often challenging in ways we could never have imagined. The more we are willing to adapt to our circumstances, the more the possibility of finding new joys and new pathways increases. This doesn't mean that these changes in our lives don't come with anguish, hardship, and tremendous emotional pain. What is born of these tribulations, however, is something akin to Jacky's story—a tale of grief, reckoning, pivoting, reconfiguring, and deep self-discovery.

I DNFed TransRockies that year, dropping out 8 miles into an intended 120-mile journey. Since I couldn't complete the race myself, I parked one to two miles up the trail each morning and greeted the runners as they journeyed into yet another tough day. Jacky's face was a compendium of smiles, hard-won athleticism, a little pain, and fierce determination as she made her way up to Hope Pass the second day and from Leadville to Camp Hale, where the tough soldiers of the 10th Mountain Division trained.

I was honored to watch Jacky complete the TransRockies three-day race, sweat-stained, tired, and triumphant, and then be immediately embraced by her loving and supportive husband and children.

We are fortunate to be able to witness Jacky living her life out loud, whether she is attempting 104 marathons in 104 days, 100 miles on a treadmill with her trusty running blade, or simply trying to get through her days without the blisters it sometimes causes.

This is a human story, one we should all take to heart and leg. And then, run.

Introduction

Marathon 102 of 104

Four months. More than 2,600 miles. Now, here I was, going one more lap around the 1.6-mile course I'd traveled hundreds of times.

It was a late afternoon in April, and the sun had warmed the dry Arizona air to the mid-eighties. I came around the dirt trail onto the cement sidewalk around the lake in Veterans Oasis Park, where locals fish for sunfish and trout in the shadow of saguaros and other succulents. As I rounded the curve, hugging the edge of the waterfront, the friends I was running with dropped back to give me space. I peered out from under the brim of my tie-dyed trucker cap and watched my family come into view.

My nine-year-old daughter, Eliza, long hair blowing in the warm breeze, held one end of a finish-line tape. At the other end stood her older brother, Dexter, a preteen whose red shirt matched his dusty Nikes. As usual, my husband, Edwin, was handling the camera in his role of coach, videographer, and hype man all in one. From behind the line, he motioned for me to stop briefly, hoping to capture the perfect shot.

I slowed but could not halt my momentum. I was about to complete a marathon-distance run for the 102nd consecutive day, a feat never before accomplished—let alone by someone running with a prosthetic. I could see the finish, and there was no stopping me.

When I embarked on this endeavor on January 1, 2022, I wasn't sure I would ever reach this point. Along the way, I also had my doubts. I got shin splints on day 11. Fatigue and strong cravings set in until I overhauled my diet on day 39. On day 100, the tread simply popped off the bottom of my carbon fiber running blade, causing me to slip around the trail. Edwin and a tube of super glue came to my rescue. (This is the story of my running life, to be honest!)

Then there was day 75, when the snap I felt was mental. I broke down by the side of the trail, my body willing, but my mind seemingly unable to let me continue. For a moment, as I crouched in the Arizona dust, I questioned my purpose. "What a dumb idea. Why did I even sign up for this?" I thought. "There's no way I can continue."

But after a bit of wallowing, I remembered how far I'd come. Even if I didn't feel it right then, I was stronger than I believed. I got up and—step by step, mile by mile—I kept going.

Now, I was mere feet from the finish line, my hands raised in victory.

~

Most people who know me now are shocked to learn that for most of my life I wasn't at all sporty. I never ran on two legs, at least not if I could help it. As a kid in South Africa, I loved being in the water and would sometimes swim a few laps in the Olympic-sized pool in my neighborhood. But on the days our gym class did laps around the track, I'd try to hide in the bathroom.

When my leg was amputated in 2002, when I was 26, to treat a rare form of cancer, Ewing sarcoma, running became an even less likely future endeavor. My countryman Oscar Pistorius—the famous (and eventually infamous) amputee and Olympic sprinter—wouldn't get his first blades until the following year. There weren't many examples of amputee runners for me to follow, even if I had been looking for them.

My diagnosis and surgery all happened so fast, in a matter of weeks, that I could barely process the loss at first. I was living in the Netherlands at the time, and while I received excellent medical care, my Dutch doctors were blunt and straightforward. I wasn't offered counseling to cope with my loss, nor would it have occurred to me to ask for it.

Edwin and I were busy sorting through the logistics of appointments and surgery, and after that, we focused on what seemed like more immediate concerns: the pain that overwhelmed me, as well as the task of learning to walk on a prosthetic with crutches, and then without them. Mental health wasn't nearly as much at the forefront of cultural conversation back then. So I simply pushed through, as I always had.

I was out of the hospital in record time, and back to work as soon as possible afterward. But though I recovered quickly physically, a part of me was still scarred and hurting. When I looked at myself, I saw only the flaws and missing pieces, so I turned away from my reflection.

I wore long pants and closed-toe shoes, and made it my mission to blend in. When my husband and I moved to the United Kingdom, and then to the United States, people who didn't know me or my backstory often had no idea I was missing a leg or had a prosthetic. Eventually, I became so good at convincing others I was just the same as them, and I could do whatever they did, that I started to believe it.

It took running—a sport I wouldn't find until decades later, in my forties—to make me realize that I was capable of far more. Not only could I learn to run with a blade, I could take it places few others dared to go: on gnarly trails, straight up icy cliffs, and to a 60-mile multistage race with 20,000 feet of ascent. (There weren't many runners competing, and I was the only amputee.) I could turn pandemic race cancelations into an opportunity to run 100 miles on a treadmill, travel 300 miles on foot from Los Angeles to Las Vegas, and spend a cold, rainy New Year's holiday taking 200-plus laps around a mile-long dirt loop. And as arduous as that all sounds, I'd actually enjoy it!

For years, I'd hid my disability and my prosthetic, in large part because people believed I couldn't do as much as someone with two healthy legs. Now, I was not only wearing shorts in public but taking on increasingly intense challenges as a sponsored athlete with a growing following.

Things don't always go perfectly, of course. I've been known to slip in the mud, get lost in the middle of trail races, or drop a piece of my equipment along the way. But each obstacle I face becomes a stepping stone. When I slide down a hill on my bum or have to stick the tread back on the bottom of my blade with Band-Aids, duct tape, or super glue, I build my tool kit and learn new ways to improvise, both of which help me to continue moving forward.

Marathon 102 of 104

I channeled all that strength as I broke through the tape held by my children and crossed the finish line of my 102nd marathon. Just to seal the deal, I'd go on to complete two more marathons in the two days after that; my official Guinness World Record certificate honors me for 104 marathon-distance runs in 104 consecutive days. But 102 was the day I officially surpassed every runner who'd gone before me.

Having crossed the line, I kept running, for just a few feet, to plant a kiss on Edwin, who was behind the camera. Then I dropped my hands to my knees, my head hanging between my legs and my blade.

He asked how I felt. "Happy," I said. "Tired." But as I shakily raised my head back up, something else swept over me: a wave of disbelief, followed by sheer awe at what I had just accomplished.

That feeling, that moment, is what changes everything. It drives me to keep doing what I do, seeking the outside edges of my untapped potential. When I encounter an unexpected barrier, it reminds me I have the courage and tools to push through. And so, I firmly believe, do you.

For amputees, physical activity of any kind can be life-changing—even life-saving—and I hope I'll encourage them to get started. But my message is for everyone, regardless of what you may perceive as your limitations. All of us are capable of far more than we realize. And if you dare to push your boundaries and do hard things, you'll learn to accept who you are, even as you surpass who you dreamed you could be.

1

FIND WHAT DRIVES YOU

Weeks Before Marathon 1 of 104

When people hear I ran 104 marathons in 104 days, they tend to have questions. One of the first is, Why?

About five years after I started running, I saw an Instagram post about Alyssa Clark, a professional trail runner and adventurer who's always taking on exciting new challenges. She had run 95 marathons in 95 consecutive days, a new Guinness World Record. Some might have found this accomplishment intimidating or unbelievable. I found it impressive, but I also wondered how someone could get to that point but then stop before finding out if they could reach 100.

By this point, I'd run several ultramarathons (anything over the 26.2-mile standard marathon length), including distances of 50-plus miles. I was intrigued to see how far I could push my body and my Fillauer Obsidian running blade. I was currently in the middle of training for the Moab 240, a grueling race covering 240 miles through Utah deserts, canyons, and mountain ranges in October. A marathon a day would give me smaller milestones to focus on as I built up my endurance for that race.

I decided to make the challenge a fundraiser for a nonprofit I'd worked with in the past, Amputee Blade Runners. I'd learned early in my running journey that adaptive and para-athletes face significant financial and logistical barriers. Running blades are expensive and often not covered by insurance. I pictured a young boy I'd met through the organization who, also an amputee, just wanted to run and play with his friends. I hoped to raise enough money to provide blades for at least two athletes like him, so I set up a GoFundMe page to collect donations. The next step was filing paperwork with Guinness World Records to let them know I was on the hunt for the title.

Then, I figured I'd better tell Edwin. I knew that running 26.2 miles daily would require some shifts in our family responsibilities and childcare. Fortunately, my husband knows me well enough to expect the unexpected. The more absurd the idea, the more likely he'd back me in tackling it, using his engineer's brain to map out the logistics. We talked through how each day might look. During the week, I'd get Dexter and Eliza off to school, then start my run. On the weekends, he'd log his own miles super early and then tag back in so I could head out, or I'd run on the treadmill instead. He and the kids would work together to help with tasks like cooking meals and doing laundry.

Not only did that arrangement make things possible, I knew it would give me yet another reason to stay committed to the goal. If I ever woke up wondering how I could get through yet another 26.2, I could think of my family and how they had shifted their lives for my off-the-wall goals. And I knew they wouldn't let me off the hook, even if I was tempted to slack off. (I could hear them now, asking after me when they got home from school: "Has Mummy done her marathon yet?")

I'd already begun to see the power of doing big things and sharing them widely. I regularly received messages about the impact I was having on others, including one note from a woman with lupus who'd been unable to run for years. Her doctors had recently changed her medication, and things were finally feeling easier for her. After watching me, she wrote, she got on her treadmill and took a few running strides—steps that meant the world to her, and to me.

After all, I could easily remember the days when I never would have dreamed of running a single step, let alone more than 100 marathons.

July 2003

Baths are supposed to be relaxing, but this one was anything but. Nineteen years before I would start planning my multi-marathon adventure, I sat in the lukewarm water, staring at my legs. Ankles, feet, calves...right now, I had two of each, and ten toes.

By this time tomorrow, half of them—part of me—would be missing.

This wasn't how my life was supposed to go. Edwin and I had met in South Africa, had been married for just about four years, and had recently moved to the Netherlands because he was offered a job there. After a childhood that was difficult at times—my parents drank heavily, and my father had what I'll kindly call "traditional" ideas about women's roles—I was now living in a new country with a husband I loved and a flourishing career in pharmaceutical marketing. I finally felt free to be myself and pursue my dreams.

But then I was diagnosed with a terrifying disease, and I was on the eve of a life-changing surgery. Now, all I wanted was to survive, to get back to the life that had turned from promising to precarious.

Just a few weeks prior, I had visited the doctor complaining about pain around an area of scar tissue in my left leg. I'd had a growth removed a few years prior and had a long scar as a result, one that almost looked like a dent in my calf. Though the growth wasn't cancerous, the spot had never really stopped hurting. Eventually, even brushing up against a piece of furniture or another person would send a bolt of pain up my leg—the type of pain that takes your breath away.

I went to my tall, gray-haired doctor several times, seeking answers and relief. He kept assuring me it was nothing to worry about. After all, I was twenty-six and perfectly healthy. Pain was normal around scar tissue, he said, looking down at me. I'd just have to learn to deal with it.

But the morning after yet another frustrating appointment, I woke up with not only pain but golf ball–sized swelling protruding from just above my ankle. I called back and once again went to his small, dark office, a space that felt like an old-school library. When I showed him the new lump, his face went pale and his eyes widened.

The medical system in the Netherlands moves efficiently, and the next week, I had a biopsy. They put me under and cut out a sizable chunk of the mass, leaving me with stitches and yet more pain. The doctor laid out a clear timeline for the results. I'd hear within four days, he said—but if it was cancer, they would call within forty-eight hours.

Those were two of the longest days of my life. I honestly don't know what diagnosis I was expecting; at that point, I saw cancer as something that happened to other people. Still, when my office phone rang on day two, I dreaded lifting the receiver. "You need to come in," the voice on the other end told me. "And bring someone with you." My heart sank as I realized that, now, it was happening to *me*.

~

Edwin and I returned the next day. The hospital was religiously affiliated, but we weren't really people of faith, so the sight of a priest in the cold, clinical room was far from reassuring. "Am I dying?" I couldn't help but wonder.

Edwin tells me I was calm when the doctor delivered the news that I did, indeed, have a malignant tumor in my leg. "No, thank you," I told the priest, who offered a prayer and a listening ear. Instead, I asked questions, listened carefully to the doctor's responses, and noted that I'd next need to visit a specialist. But when I think back on that appointment, I remember nothing after the word "cancer." The rest of the conversation is a black box, locked tight in my memory.

I do recall that just after we walked out toward the parking lot, I burst into tears. "Why is this happening?" I wailed. "What did I do wrong to deserve this?" I generally tried to be a good person, although of course I'd talked back to my parents some as a kid and still had a bit of a potty mouth. But surely the occasional curse word wasn't worthy of such cruel payback. Edwin is a problem-solver by nature, usually eager to pinpoint the cause of an issue and recommend a solution. In this case, even he was at a loss for words.

Suddenly, I didn't want to talk about it anymore, didn't even want to think about it. All I wanted was to focus on something, anything, else. We agreed we would both go back to work. As bizarre as it was, I stuffed my emotions down and returned to my desk as if nothing had happened.

The next week, we went to see Antoni Taminiau, a professor and expert in treating sarcoma, at Leiden University Medical Center. Edwin was reassured—here was one of the foremost authorities on this disease in all of Europe. We were definitely lucky to see him, but I felt far from fortunate when he sat me down and, with that typical Dutch bluntness, said, "Well, you've got Ewing sarcoma, and the only solution is amputation."

"Amputation? Whaaaa?" I figured we'd be talking about chemo, maybe radiation. Instead, by the end of that week, I had an appointment to have my leg removed.

Ewing sarcoma is a rare but extremely aggressive cancer that forms mainly in the bones and soft tissue. It accounts for about 1 percent of childhood cancers, often striking preteens, teens, and young adults during puberty, when their bones are growing. It's very rare among adults, and even less common among women compared to men. Medical experts still don't really know why it occurs, other than that it's a random gene mutation rather than being an inherited trait passed down through families.

If I was looking for answers to the question "Why me?," the doctor wouldn't be providing them. He was, however, clear on our next steps. Ewing sarcoma spreads quickly, and when it does, it typically goes to the lungs. If he took out only the tumor, the risk of metastasis was much greater; plus, he'd have to remove so much of my leg muscle that I wouldn't have control of my foot and would have to use a wheelchair. Amputation offered my best chance at not only a cancer-free future but the likelihood of walking again, with a prosthetic.

My leg or my life. I suppose it wasn't really that difficult of a decision. Still, my mind reeled. In the span of a week, I'd received a potentially fatal diagnosis and learned the treatment would be life-altering.

The week before my surgery was full of more tests and waiting and anxiety. Doctors had to make sure that the cancer hadn't already spread. I had MRIs and a full-body scan, all of which fortunately came back clear. It was such a weird time, a roller coaster of emotions. When I got the results, I felt relief in knowing that the disease was contained and treatment would work. I thought about how the cancer would be gone and that my chances of survival were relatively high.

But sitting in that bath the night before, I was hit with a wave of grief for myself and my body. A voice inside me said, "Tomorrow, you're going to be different. You're going to be ugly." Tears slid down my cheeks and into the bathwater. I watched them disappear, realizing the next time I sat here, an entire limb would be invisible as well.

~

No one warns you that amputation hurts more than you could imagine. At times, I just wanted to be put out of my misery. The morphine pump they gave me couldn't keep up with the pain. During my hospital stay, I wound up in the emergency room twice for extra pain relief injections.

I went home after six days, much faster than expected. I was proud of my swift progress and glad to be in my own space, but at home, of course, there were no more emergency epidurals. When the pain breaks through, you learn to breathe into it, accepting that you can't escape. You simply must carry it with you, like a dark secret, learning along the way that you can move forward despite its searing presence.

Then there are the phantom feelings in the missing limb. At times, I leaned over to scratch an itch on my left big toe, but there wasn't anything there. I'd also get the sensation that my toes were cramped and crossed over each other. I can't even tell you how freaky this felt. I had no idea how to relieve those feelings. Eventually, I learned that I could massage certain parts of my stump, and that seemed to calm the nerve signals that were still trying to fire into the missing tissue. But that would take time to figure out. At first, I struggled.

As I made my way around on crutches, I kept encountering new challenges: Getting out of bed to go to the bathroom. Standing over the stove to make dinner. Getting up and down the stairs of our row house to the bedroom, where I remained determined to sleep despite the difficulty. (I crawled up the stairs and slid down them.) At one point, sheer anger gripped me. I can recall standing outside the front door on the sidewalk, wobbling a bit and looking to the sky. I shouted up at a higher power I didn't even believe in, "What the hell did I do wrong?!" I still couldn't shake the notion that this was some sort of punishment, and I demanded to know how I'd earned it. Of course, the heavens had no more answers than Edwin or my doctors.

As I was recovering, Dr. Taminiau mentioned the South African swimmer Natalie du Toit. When she was seventeen, she was hit by a car while riding her scooter after swimming practice. Her leg was amputated at the knee, but before she could walk again, she was back in the pool. The same year I lost my leg, 2002, she competed against swimmers without disabilities in the 800-meter race at the All-Africa Games (now called the Africa Games)—and won. Just five years later, she went to Beijing and became the first female amputee to compete in the Olympic Games.

Dr. Taminiau also told me about another of his patients, a snowboarder who was able to return to the slopes with her prosthetic. At the time, I was more of a casual exerciser, someone who biked indoors to stay fit or outdoors for transportation. But learning about these athletes gave me something to strive for and assured me there was life on the other side of amputation. I posted a newspaper article about Natalie behind my bed as I recovered, to remind me.

~

At first I had regular scans every month, and then every two months, to make sure the cancer didn't reappear. Other people sitting in the hospital waiting room were clearly in the middle of chemo, their hair, bodies, and spirits thinned by the potent cocktail of cancer-killing drugs. Many huddled in fear, clearly anticipating the worst news from their next rounds of tests. It was guaranteed I'd cry every time I saw other patients frightened and fighting for their lives.

These visits filled me with anxiety and grief, but also, bit by bit, they shifted my perspective. Unlike many of the other patients, I was making progress. The cancer wasn't spreading, and I didn't need harsh treatments that would continue harming healthy cells in my body. Week by week, as my wound healed, the burden of pain grew ever-so-slightly lighter.

And most importantly of all, I was alive. There were plenty of hard days and difficult feelings ahead. But the seeds of gratitude and grit that would eventually take me across finish lines were planted.

~

Survival is a powerful motivator. When it feels like everything's falling apart around you, sometimes the best you can do is hang on for dear life. Examples of others who have prevailed through similar circumstances can help you tap into your deepest reserves of hope and resilience. And channeling gratitude turns your focus away from what's lost and toward what remains and what's possible.

I've learned this through experience, but research backs me up. Scientists have found that people going through bone marrow transplants were less anxious and depressed, and had a better quality of life, if they scored highly on a gratitude questionnaire. A literature review also suggests that, after surviving cancer, grateful people are more likely to experience what's called post-traumatic growth. That means they feel stronger, have warmer connections and relationships, and overall feel a greater appreciation for life because of what they've been through. In a study of nearly five hundred athletes, those who said they were grateful for what their sport had brought to their lives were less likely to get burned out on the activity. And University of Oregon researchers found that when women wrote in an online gratitude journal for just three weeks, their brains physically changed, rewiring in a way that turned them more toward generosity and altruism.

I don't have a formal practice like journaling or writing gratitude lists, but I know that works for many people. I keep it simple with a mental inventory of things I'm thankful for. At the top of that list are my family and my running. My husband has stayed by my side through the toughest moments. Even when Dexter storms into his room without a word after school or Eliza asks, one more time, if we'll buy her a horse, my kids bring me joy. My running has taken me all over the country and the world, allowing me to do things that other amputees—and people without disabilities too—can't (or won't) do.

And most of all, I survived cancer, when many others do not. All it cost me was my leg.

When I hit a tough moment during a race or a training run, I remind myself of all these big things, and the little ones too. Marathon number 83 of 104 was a brutal one; temperatures topped 110°F, and the fatigue of the effort was starting to build. Each time I found myself tempted to quit, I shifted my focus. The sun was bright, but beautiful. Rabbits and roadrunners scurried out of my way. My friend Rachel had voluntarily chosen to suffer with me, and we passed the time talking about old movies or simply sweating in silence. And when I shuffled toward a seven-hour finish, I gave thanks to my body for allowing me the opportunity to try.

~

If you find yourself in a tough situation, eventually you may realize you're through the roughest part of a particular rapid. As you reflect on how far you've come and the strength you've gained in the process, you might begin to wonder if you can harness that strength to keep pushing further. This sense of curiosity and exploration—the force that prompted me to ask, "Why not me?" when I read about Alyssa Clark—can take you to incredible places...if you let it.

As my running journey has progressed, I've felt an even stronger pull to use my good fortune to benefit others. Two years after my marathon record, to celebrate the twenty-first anniversary of becoming cancer-free, I decided to run at least 21 kilometers—13.1 miles—every day for 250 days. I called it Project "I Can Do Hard Things." In so many of my tougher moments on the roads and trails, I remind myself of all I've been through. Over the years, I've whispered the same mantra to myself when I felt my confidence lagging: "You can do hard things." And as I did, the voice grew louder and more definitive. "I can do hard things," I told myself, and I believed it. I even got it tattooed on my arm, a permanent reminder of my strength.

My goal with Project "I Can Do Hard Things" was to run 5,250 kilometers (more than 3,200 miles). That number—5,250—represents the number of people in the United States who are diagnosed with cancer every day. Along the way, I would raise money for the Sarcoma Foundation of America. Though the goal was at least a half marathon each day for 250 days, I naturally snuck a few ultramarathons into the schedule too. By the time I finished—on April 6, 2024—I'd run 7,055 kilometers, or 4,384 miles.

Most importantly, I dedicated each day's run to someone whose life was touched by cancer. When you're diagnosed with such a fearsome disease, it can feel like you're dealing with it alone; even if you have a support team around you, it's hard to find others who can truly understand or identify with your emotions. Sometimes, stigma can stop you from sharing your story and letting people in. And when cancer claims someone close to you, it can feel like the whole world stops while you're frozen in grief. I wanted my runs to be a way to invite other people to take the time and space to reflect, process their feelings, and honor those who'd passed away.

I asked people who had been affected by cancer to message me or comment on my Instagram account with stories about themselves or loved ones. The responses I got floored me. One young woman told me about the man she was supposed to marry; he was diagnosed with Ewing sarcoma and died just before their wedding day. Peggy and Jordan, a mother and son, died of cancer eight years apart, and I ran for them on day 83. Day 85, on October 24, was especially personal. I ran in honor of Alexandra Wolf, a friend and fellow amputee who'd lost her battle with sarcoma days earlier.

I kept the names in a spreadsheet, along with a few details about their stories. With Edwin's help, I created a template of a race bib with the mantra "You can do hard things" on top and the name and story of the person I was running for underneath. Each time I headed out the door, I pinned it to the back of my hydration vest, a reminder of how fleeting and precious life can be.

Sometimes, friends and family members joined me. One woman who came to run with me toward the middle of the project told me her mom had been battling cancer in silence. She was embarrassed, thinking others would view her illness as a weakness. But after noticing what I was doing, shedding light on the people affected by the disease, she'd begun opening up to her friends, family members, and colleagues. The support she received in return brightened her outlook—and she wished she'd shared sooner. Another woman joined me in memory of her dad, who'd died of sarcoma. As we ran, she told me all about him—how kind he was to her, and how much she missed him.

Many of the days were heavy. To shoulder the burdens, I drew inspiration from the mission. I'm so lucky, I realized, that I get to do this—not just to run but to bear witness to the struggles others have been through. Those emotions and experiences aren't easy to share. People trusted me with their fears and sadness, the memories they hoped would always live on. I felt a responsibility to keep going, both with this challenge and, in the bigger picture, in this sport.

There were bright spots too—like day 111, when I ran for Julia Becker Collins. She was already an ultrarunner when she began fighting thyroid cancer three years prior. Since her diagnosis, she'd completed another seven ultras. And then there was Owen Boyle, who I ran for on day 78. He was diagnosed with Ewing sarcoma in 2022, after his freshman year in high school, when a foot he broke at a soccer tournament wouldn't heal. He did chemo and had what's called a Syme amputation, where doctors remove the foot at the ankle. As he recovered, he returned as the manager for his team, the Wolfpack. Two years later, in April 2024, he returned to the soccer field with his prosthetic.

Maybe you're in a place or time when it feels like you can't see past the next day—or even the next hour, or the next minute. Perhaps it's all you can do to bear your own pain, to breathe deeply into your greatest fears, to simply live to see another moment. I've been there, during my battle with cancer and many times afterward. When I am, I do my best to find even the smallest of bright spots until the darkness lifts.

As the light grows, I'm not content to bask in its glow. We can't stop bad things from happening to ourselves or to other people, but we can use the strength we gain from surviving our worst days to explore a better future. What could you do if you used that resilience to push the boundaries and try something that scares you? Can you use it to fuel new goals that take you places you might not have imagined you could go—and bring others along with you?

2

STAY OPEN TO ADVENTURE

Days Before Marathon 1 of 104

The more I began to pull together my triple-digit marathon plans, the more excited I felt. Yes, it was a lot of running, a daunting prospect. But digging more into Alyssa Clark's story inspired me. She'd run her first 100-mile race—the HURT100 in Hawaii—three years prior, at age twenty-three, and made the podium. Since then, she'd claimed victory at the Ouray 100-mile race in Colorado and set a fastest known time, or FKT—the term for a speed record set outside of an official race or event along a given route—on the 350-mile Pinhoti Trail.

She impressed the hell out of me, and I wanted to see if an amputee could match her significant achievement. I even reached out to her as I started to make my plans, seeking input on how to gather data for a Guinness World Record. She was kind and helpful—all about supporting another female runner.

Even with her support, however, I didn't know for sure whether this was possible for me. To be honest, a part of me didn't believe I'd make it past ten days. And when I started to share my goal with others, they seemed to have a similar feeling. My brother, Lionel, and one of my best running friends, Jeannette, clearly thought I was crazy. My sponsors were kind but noncommittal, telling me it was an interesting goal and then suggesting I check back in once the project was underway.

But inside, I recognized that familiar flicker, a combination of anxiety and anticipation, that always lets me know I'm on track toward a goal worth pursuing. Yes, I knew, this could all blow up in my face. But cancer had taught me that life was prone to doing that anyway. Running had shown me I could learn new ways to navigate the challenges. My life was richer for all the chances I'd taken—the new countries we'd moved to, the start lines I'd toed, the times I'd turned doubt into doing. And the more I ran, the less content I was to stay in my comfort zone.

On Friday, January 14, I made it social-media official. "I will attempt to run a marathon every day for 100 days," I wrote, "starting Monday." There was no going back now.

~

When Edwin and I first met, at a bar in South Africa where he was working, I was drawn to his long hair, a sign of rebellion that spoke to me. He remembers my laugh. His day job was as an apprentice at a telecommunications company, making him among the few people to have a cell phone in 1994. He wrote his number on my arm, and I called him a few days later. Before long, we were inseparable.

One thing that bound us from the beginning is our passion for going to new places and trying new things. Edwin's Dutch father, an engineer on a ship, had often taken his wife with him as he sailed around the world before they had kids, so Edwin grew up with parents who had traveled to places like Japan, Australia, and Canada in the 1950s—a time when working-class people weren't typically globe-trotting. They eventually settled in South Africa, where Edwin was born, and although they didn't travel as much for work, they still took him and his brother and sister on frequent trips. Adventure was in his blood from the start.

For me, the drive to explore came more from a need to escape and define the contours of my own life. My dad wasn't necessarily a fan of women having jobs or dreams beyond motherhood and family. My parents rarely left Pretoria, where we lived on the grounds of the prison where my father worked. I dreamed of a bigger life—maybe I'd be a dog trainer or work in business, professions that he told me were only for men. To be myself, I knew I'd need to get away.

And together, Edwin and I flew. When we got married, his uncle was living in the Netherlands. It was 1998, and companies were recruiting employees to help prepare for Y2K, the set of software issues that everyone feared would arise when the calendar rolled from 1999 to 2000. Edwin was offered a consulting role in the

Netherlands, and we jumped at the chance to start the next chapter six thousand miles away.

That was our first big move, and it started our general philosophy on relocating: to adapt. We aim to connect with the locals and live as they do, immersing ourselves so we can get up to speed. In the Netherlands, we went to a Dutch school to learn the language. Everyone there cycles for transportation, so we got on bikes as quickly as we could. I can still remember my first trip to the supermarket on two wheels—I was so excited that I filled up the bags on the back of my bike to the point that getting home was a struggle. I laughed and realized I'd have to pack lighter the next time, spacing out heavier items like milk, melons, and laundry detergent.

When we lived in Europe, we took the chance to roam widely around the continent. We both traveled for work, and when our destinations differed, we'd find a fun place to meet in the middle. For instance, when I flew to Seattle and he was in Vancouver, we met up for our first-ever Canadian holiday. Once, when Edwin was between two consulting gigs, we packed the car and spent two and a half months on the road, hopping from city to city and country to country. If we liked a place, we stayed for a week (or more); if we didn't enjoy the vibe, we moved on. With nothing planned, we saw so much—historic churches, cozy villages, the French coastline in Nice. We finished with two weeks spent camping in a two-person tent in Corsica, a gorgeous Italian island in the Mediterranean.

When you step across the border of a new country, so much instantly changes. The stores, the road signs, the local clothing and customs. I loved seeing what the grocery stores were called in

Germany, the types of restaurants locals dined at in Italy, and how people did (or didn't) use their towels to claim chairs by swimming pools in France. Eventually, we were able to figure out where people were from based on small differences in clothing or behavior—say, the volume of their voices or whether they wore socks with their flip-flops.

But for all those differences, there are always common threads. One morning in Paris, we were getting ready to leave our room when a hotel staff member came by to clean it. We didn't speak French, and she didn't speak English. But we still managed to sustain a ten-minute conversation entirely made up of pointing and other gestures. I saw the same thing the first time we took Dexter and Eliza to South Africa to meet their cousins, who speak only Afrikaans. Though my kids spoke only English, language was no barrier to them becoming the best of friends as they played together.

Absorbing yourself in each new culture, you begin to realize that while everyone does things a little bit differently, people largely want the same things: a safe place to live and a good life for themselves and their family. The things that make us different pale compared to those that unite us. For Edwin and me, staying true to our sense of adventure has always opened up new ideas, experiences, and ways of thinking and living. But it has also anchored us to the values that we return to time and again, including community, connection, and helping each other through the rough patches to find a way forward.

My cancer diagnosis and amputation did throw a wrench in my wanderings, at least for a little while. Everything was more challenging at first, and travel was no exception. My prosthetic leg would inevitably set off the security alarm at the airport, and because I always wore long pants, it took some time to explain why. I'd frequently get swabbed for explosives or have to stand awkwardly on one leg while they put my prosthetic through the scanner. As everyone stared, my face turned red and my palms would get sweaty. Often, security officers treated me as if I'd committed a crime, aggressively ordering me around and searching me. Once, in Malta, I was escorted to a separate room to remove both my pants and my leg. It was all so humiliating. (I'm happy to report that times have changed a lot since then, and travel is much less tricky now. But I do always wear shorts to the airport these days so people can tell, right away, that I have a prosthetic. Getting out in front of the questions is now my philosophy!)

And these experiences while traveling weren't the only reminder that, even as I grew more capable and confident in using my prosthetic leg, others saw me differently. When we moved to the United Kingdom and I began looking for a job, I applied at a pharmaceutical company for a role in event management. I'd made it to the second round and was interviewing with one of the managers on the team. After some discussion of my skills and experience, I mentioned my disability, in part to make it clear that I was a strong, resilient person and a hard worker. "I survived cancer—I can meet any challenge," I told him.

I was entirely unprepared for what he asked next: "So if we were to employ you, what if there was a fire or another emergency? What would you do to get out the door?"

My first reaction was confusion. What did he mean? I'd walked into the room on my perfectly functional prosthetic. "I…I would just run out the door?" I stammered.

I could see him mentally calculating, his brows furrowing. Did he think I would have to somehow hop on one leg to escape? Have someone else carry me? I don't know where his mind was going, but needless to say, I no longer wanted to work for him.

Afterward, I rehashed the interaction again and again in my mind, crafting all the comebacks I could've offered. "I'd phone for a cab," I should have said, or, "I'd parachute out the window." And if something like that were to happen now, I'd probably even have the confidence to challenge him. Heck, I might even have walked into the interview in a skirt and cracked a joke about losing my leg in a poker game before he even said "hello."

But at the time, I berated myself for opening my mouth at all. What was I thinking? I should have stuck to my typical plan: wear long pants, walk as confidently as possible, never let anyone know about my amputation unless they absolutely needed to.

~

In the early years after my amputation, I did try to stay active for my mental and physical health. When we moved to North Carolina in 2015, I went to spin classes at the local YMCA once or twice a week. In fact, that was the one place I didn't wear long pants. I arrived, headed to the locker room, and slipped into capris that covered the top of my knee but not my full leg. There were still limits to my boldness—I always slid into the back row of bikes and returned to my armor of jeans or sweatpants before I stepped outside the gym doors—but I noticed that, in a space where everyone was focused on their own bodies, mine felt slightly more anonymous and safe.

Edwin, meanwhile, was hard-core into running by this point. It was something new for him: He'd played rugby as a kid and a bit of squash as an adult, but as we moved from the Netherlands to the United Kingdom and started having children, the combination of work and parenting left him with little time for movement.

Not long after Eliza was born and Edwin turned forty, he started thinking about his health and his life. He realized that if he wanted to see her grow up and graduate and get married, he needed to take better care of his body by exercising. He found the gym boring, and running was the simplest (and, at the time, least expensive) alternative. He joined a couple of buddies from work who ran at lunchtime, jogging by landmarks such as the Tower Bridge and the Tower of London.

At first, his knees ached whenever he reached around the 5K mark. But after reading the book *Born to Run* by Christopher McDougall, he switched to running shoes with a lower "drop," meaning a smaller difference in height between the heel and the toe. Lower-drop shoes aren't necessarily right for everyone—any experienced runner can tell you that shoe fit and preference is highly personal—but for him, they were magic, at least once he built up the calf strength to support the difference in strain on his Achilles tendon.

I was happy for him, but I can't say I truly understood the appeal of running at first. I watched the long hours of effort he put in on the weekends and the loads of dirty laundry he toted home from the office each week. The whole thing sounded exhausting. Could a T-shirt and a tiny race medal be worth it? I was content with my trips to the gym and my spin bike, regardless of how my prosthetic pinched the back of my knee as I pedaled.

Still, I did my best to be the supportive spouse he'd always been for me. I was happy to see him doing something that made him feel good. When he started racing, I showed up to cheer as often as I could, bringing the kids when I could.

Of course, as Edwin does, he pushed himself to progress. He worked his way methodically from 5K to 10K to a half marathon, and then he signed up for a full 26.2-mile trail run, the South Downs Marathon, in 2015. Early in the morning the day of that race, I packed up the kids and headed to the finish line, in a hilly, picturesque park west of London. I had little sense of Edwin's pace or how long it would take him to cover the distance, and most races didn't have tracking at the time. (It's still uncommon at smaller events on the trails.) Fearing I'd miss him, we arrived hours early, which gave the kids *plenty* of time to complain about how cold they were.

Scanning for Edwin's glasses and flop of brown hair, I watched as runners finished. Some looked triumphant, others drained. Many who were clearly fatigued found an extra ounce of effort to push across the finish line. In the moments afterward, they radiated a mix of relief, exhaustion, and pride.

For whatever reason, there seemed to be a lot of dads running that day. Kids squealed and the men beamed as families reunited in giant, sweaty hugs. When Edwin finally came into view, after nearly four and a half hours of effort, Dexter and Eliza lit up like Christmas trees. They rushed to meet him meters before the line, and the three of them crossed together. From my spot on the sidelines, I began to suspect those wee medals represented something much larger.

~

When we moved from London to North Carolina in 2015, the sport anchored Edwin in our new community. Once again, he joined the running club at work. Soon, he was leading it, coaching other athletes toward achieving their goals. His own goals grew more ambitious as well: He ran a faster marathon, then qualified for the Boston Marathon and ran that too. The next logical step, he thought, was ultra distances beyond 26.2 miles, which were often held on the trails. That made me even more intrigued. I wondered what he saw in the woods on those trails, what he thought about, during all those long runs. How would he put the puzzle pieces of training together to succeed on race day?

Most of our new American friends were training for something too, and these competitions were always a topic of conversation. When we'd get together, though, they all assumed Edwin was the only athlete in the family, never bringing me into discussions about their weekly mileage or what races were ahead on their calendars. I was both miffed about being left out and curious about the possibility of joining in, my stubborn and adventurous streaks intertwining to steer me toward a new endeavor. Everyone else was setting and achieving athletic goals. Why not me? It was true that I'd never seen another amputee at any of Edwin's races. But maybe, just maybe, I could be one of the first.

Finally, I'd had enough of wondering. The Y had a running club of its own, on an indoor track that circled the top of the basketball court. It couldn't have been more than one-tenth of a mile around. That's where I first put my walking leg to the test in a few short jogs.

If you're not an amputee, you might be surprised by the idea of needing a specific limb for each activity. However, biomechanically, running and walking involve very different forces and movements, so it helps to have a prosthetic designed for the right undertaking. When you run, the muscles and tendons of your feet—cushioned by the foam of your running shoes—absorb some of the impact of landing, then return it to you as you push forward into the next step. None of that happens with a walking leg, which is all I had at first. Instead, I felt like I had bricks tied to the bottom of my shoe, and I was dragging them along behind me. I can't say it felt great.

But I hadn't been a runner before my amputation. I could tell this early attempt wasn't smooth or easy, but I hadn't yet experienced anything different, so I didn't yet know how different it *could* be with the right prosthetic. All I knew was that a spark had been lit, and it compelled me to push through the discomfort. I had one leg, and one life; I grew determined to make them work for me.

I signed up for my first 5K in the summer of 2016. The race was right there in my neighborhood, in Cary, North Carolina, so we didn't even have to drive to the start line. I put on black three-quarter-length tights, laced up a pair of white sneakers, and, at age forty-one, pinned my first-ever race bib onto my white tank top.

To say the experience of running a race with a prosthetic was humbling would be an understatement. I didn't know how much I didn't know. Each prosthetic leg has three parts: the foot that touches the ground, the liner that slides over your stump, and the socket that connects the two. I use a suction system for running now, but at the time, I used only a pin lock system, in which a pin screwed into the bottom part of the liner inserts into a shuttle lock in the socket. For me, it wasn't quite as secure as would have been ideal; my stump slid around as I ran, and the pin repeatedly poked into my skin, tearing it apart.

For a while, I wasn't even sure I could finish. I had to stop halfway through and pull my leg off to ease the pain and inspect the damage. Of course, I couldn't bear to do this in full view of the other runners. Showing my stump to the world made me feel vulnerable and naked, as if I were dropping not only my socket but also my tights. I hobbled off the course to a nearby bench. Edwin handed me a towel to shield myself. I took off my leg and surveyed the situation. The skin was shredded, and the silicon liner was full of blood. I dumped out the liner, wiped it (and myself) off, put everything on again, and got back out there.

Besides that stop, there was also a hell of a lot of walking. My face turned beet red, and I could feel myself leaning over from the effort.

I could barely breathe as I dragged my body, and my leg, around the course. But despite the blood and the pain, I finished, and felt rather chuffed with myself as a result. At first I thought, "Never again." But as the days went by and my skin began to heal, I realized I wanted to take another shot. I'd do better with the proper equipment, I reasoned.

At that point, I started researching running blades online. I didn't know anything about them other than what I'd seen on TV, when Oscar Pistorius competed in the Olympics. I saw that there were several options, but all of them were pricey, at least $10,000. When I next had an appointment with my prosthetist, I brought it up. He'd once been a runner himself, so he had an idea of what I would need—starting with a doctor's referral, which would allow him to submit a request to my insurance company. He also had some words of warning: "Many insurance plans won't cover anything beyond a basic walking leg," he told me. "They view any specialized equipment as a so-called luxury item."

"Whaaaa?" I said, confused and enraged. I didn't see my health and fitness as an indulgence or extravagance. In some countries—for example, back in the UK—amputees could receive active prosthetics (although not always the top-of-the-line models) through the National Health Service. Here in the United States, I could have access to any blade I wanted...provided I could pay up. If only there were a better balance, where *all* amputees could have affordable, functional equipment that would keep them moving and healthy. In the meantime, even with a generous corporate insurance plan, we would have to pay the entire cost ourselves.

~

Once I'd tasted a bit of the freedom running could bring, though, I knew I wanted to continue. Unfortunately, the prosthetist was correct in guessing that our insurance company would deem even the most inexpensive running blade "inessential," but we were fortunate enough to be able to afford it out of pocket. And given my prosthetist's history with running, I felt confident in his ability to guide me through the process of fitting a blade.

And indeed, it was quite a process. Because my new foot—the Freedom Innovations Catapult—required a suction socket rather than a pin, I had to start from scratch with a whole new system. The prosthetist measured my leg many times and placed a plaster cast around my stump to mold the test socket. Once the test socket arrived, I had to try it out before my permanent socket was made.

As I began this process, I did another race, the Run for Liberty in Cary. I still struggled with my walking foot, especially because this was a trail race with uneven terrain. The looped course in a local park, which I had to cover twice, included rolling hills over dirt and grass, and there were moments when I wobbled a bit. But already, I was beginning to feel slightly more confident in my ability. I did walk some, but I didn't have to stop this time. I finished in 35 minutes and 47 seconds, a pace of 11 minutes, 31 seconds per mile.

After about three weeks, I got the call I'd been waiting for: My test socket was in. My adventure was truly about to begin.

The blade I use now looks similar to those you might have seen on Pistorius or on Paralympians such as Scout Bassett and Hunter Woodhall. The carbon fiber attaches to the socket behind my stump and then bends back a bit before arching under, a slightly tilted L shape that compresses and then expands as I stride.

But my first-ever blade, the Catapult, was a bit less streamlined. The foot was secured by a pylon directly at the bottom of the socket, at the base of my stump. From there, two springs spanned the distance between my leg and the ground. The main spring curved back like a reverse C, the bottom covered with a rubberized tread for traction. The second, supporting spring jutted straight down from the top of the foot to the bottom, creating a diagonal line across the semicircle of the C-spring.

I'll never forget the feeling of running on that blade for the first time. The first few steps were downright terrifying. When I first started walking on a prosthetic, I had to learn to trust the idea that something outside of me would support my entire weight, that I could lean into it with my full force. Now, I had to have faith that this collection of graphite and screws could hold up to the added impact of running. Talk about a leap into the unknown!

After some initial unsteadiness, I summoned all the determination my fledgling athletic career had already brought me. I took one tentative bound, then another. Suddenly, I was not just jogging but fully running. Before, I'd been lumbering along, unable to truly use the leg speed that I had. Now, I felt like I was flying.

Edwin, as always the thoughtful documentarian, filmed my first few steps. Eliza, age three at the time, put on her light-pink leotard and tutu and ran behind me. As she looked up at me with pride, a whole new world opened up in front of me.

~

I was supposed to try the test socket for a week or two and then report back. Once your permanent socket is made, no further adjustments are possible, so it's important to make sure it fits properly.

Because it's meant for a trial run, the test socket is made from high-performance plastic rather than carbon. It's stable enough to hold the runner's weight, but it isn't designed to last forever. There's always a chance it could snap. The prosthetist told me to test it for a week but not to do anything foolish.

Well, they hadn't quite learned that Jacky's definitions of "foolish" or "over the top" were different from everyone else's. I took that test socket and ran another cross-country 5K race. Despite the uneven trail—a surface not recommended for the Catapult—I felt more confident. Freed of the load I'd been dragging, I began to truly push myself. My time improved to just under 27 minutes.

I was hooked. When my permanent socket arrived—patterned in the leopard print I'd selected—I set out to make sure I was getting my $10,000 worth. I did several more 5Ks, then set my sights on a 10K race in nearby Durham that December.

When I went to pick up my packet the day before the race, that little glimmer of excitement, that thirst for adventure, bubbled up. At the time, the event—called Race 13.1 Durham—also featured a 5K and a half marathon. I asked a volunteer if I could change distances. I'm sure he assumed I wanted to drop down to the 5K. But no, I explained, I wanted to upgrade to the half marathon. What was the difference, really, between 6 miles and 13.1 miles? It didn't seem that large. I decided to find out.

Edwin the pragmatist tried to warn me about getting too greedy. "You can't do that. You didn't train for it!" he exclaimed. He was right, of course; the longest I'd run was about 6 miles. But he didn't pressure me, figuring I'd need to learn from my own mistakes.

Race morning was frigid, especially for North Carolina: around 23°F. I wasn't used to the chill and wasn't sure what to wear. I put on my trusty three-quarter tights, the single long-sleeved running shirt I owned, a headband, and a pair of gloves.

I remember feeling a sense of calm and purpose at the starting line. There were no time goals or expectations. I was here to test myself and my blade, to see what would happen if I hit the 6-mile mark and kept going.

And that's exactly what I did. We wound through Durham neighborhoods and parks, over rolling hills. With no idea of exactly how I should pace myself, I went with the flow, listening to my body and taking it all in. More than once, I thought about how frozen I was and then picked up my speed in order to get out of the cold sooner. Once the finish line was in view, I saw a woman ahead of me, and my competitive instincts kicked in. I pushed hard, passed her, and finished in just over 2 hours and 6 minutes.

This time, Edwin and the kids were waiting at the finish line for *me*. Once again, my face was bright red and I could barely breathe—but this time it was because I'd left it all out on the course, sprinting to the finish.

"You smashed it!" Edwin said with surprise and delight as he wrapped me in my puffy coat. He'd realized the mistake wasn't mine, in wanting to try the longer race, but his, in underestimating me. Though I still couldn't quite warm up, I didn't want to leave, and so we stayed, cheering on the other runners as I basked in our collective accomplishment. I thought about how, in less than a year, I'd gone from the indoor track to the 5K to more than four times that distance. Perhaps limits were even more arbitrary than I'd imagined. What others could I shatter in the months and years ahead?

Time and again in my running career, I've heard the call of adventure and answered it. I'll discover an event that piques my interest—a trail ultramarathon, a 240-mile trek across the desert, a 300-mile journey from Los Angeles to Las Vegas—and just feel in my bones that I need to give it a go. Sometimes, all it takes is filling out a registration form and my credit card number. In other cases, I have to be more persistent. Take, for instance, the Speed Project, the LA–to–Las Vegas run I did in 2025. I first had to connect with the race director on social media, then go through a top-secret vetting process to even be considered.

In other cases, adventure comes knocking on my door. In the fall of 2024, I got an Instagram message from Brent Silkey, a pastor and runner who'd been following me for a while. He runs a nonprofit, 30 for Freedom, dedicated to ending sex trafficking. He was putting together a team to take on the Great World Race—seven marathons on seven continents in seven days, slated for November 2025—and wondered if I'd want to be a part of it. My first reaction was disbelief, but once I realized he was serious and had sponsors lined up to cover the significant costs, I was all in.

Each time I commit to these outlandish adventures, I truly don't know if I'll be able to finish—but that's part of the point. Growth doesn't happen when we stick to the script or shrink from new endeavors. The hard things we choose to do empower us to face the struggles that we didn't exactly sign up for, and vice versa.

Trust me, if it were an option, I'd have tried to cancel having cancer! But persevering through that challenge gave me the skills and resilience I use in every race. And all those moments on the journey in between—the drives around Europe, the bike rides to the grocery store, the friends who've seen me at my best and my worst as they've crewed my ultra races—that make the effort all worth it.

I fully realize that not everyone gets excited by running hundreds or thousands of miles. Please recall that I'm the girl who hid in the school bathroom rather than finish a single lap during gym class! So while these might not be the specific challenges that speak to you, I trust that there's an adventurer of some sort inside you, begging to be recognized. Pay attention to those little twinges of envy or excitement that arise when you're scrolling social media, meeting new people at a party, or watching the morning news. When someone—be it an athlete, an activist, or an artist—has done something that fills you with awe and admiration, it just might be worth asking why you can't follow in their footsteps. Yes, you may find it equal parts thrilling and terrifying; you might not be sure you have what it takes to prevail. But the only certainty is that if you don't try, you'll never know.

3

PLAN WHAT YOU CAN, THEN TAKE THE LEAP

Marathon 1 of 104

After I announced my plan to run 100 consecutive marathons on Friday, Monday came quickly. It was time to go. I decided to start marathon number 1 right in my Gilbert, Arizona, neighborhood, making small loops around the roads where the pavement was smooth and predictable.

You might think I'd use this opportunity to explore new routes in the Arizona mountains, but while that idea sounded appealing at first, I quickly realized it could backfire. As I started to picture the enormity of what I was undertaking—100 marathons in 100 consecutive days, a casual 2,620 miles—I decided that, in some important ways, I needed to think small.

Every race represents a balancing act—managing the parts that are in your control, knowing that at some point, you simply must step into the unknown. When an event stretches for hundreds of miles and sometimes multiple days across uneven terrain, you can't predict how your body and mind will react. A minor stumble at mile 10 can cause a domino effect of pain that becomes nearly unbearable by mile 95. Blisters can pop up where you've never had them before. Somewhere around one-third of ultrarunners experience hallucinations at some point during a long race. I have personally hallucinated snakes on the trail during the Moab 240. And at the Across the Years 200-mile run, I mistook large boulders for sheep.

To add to this, I have more variables to consider than most runners do. Without an ankle, it's harder for me to feel my way across bumps in the trail. Mud and water can make the tread on my blade even more slippery than it usually is. I'm also not exactly blessed with a great sense of direction. A self-directed marathon could easily become an all-day expedition if I got lost on a new trail.

So, I stayed close to home, where I was never far from food, water, or facilities. Dexter and Eliza's elementary school was less than a half mile away, and I thought it might be fun to run past and get occasional waves from the kiddos through the window or from the playground at recess.

I didn't really worry about getting sick of the same small loop. Keep in mind, I'm a person who's run almost twenty-four hours straight on a treadmill. I'm not afraid of a little monotony. Keeping it simple meant I could zone out instead of worrying about missing a turn, and I also wouldn't have to haul around in an overloaded hydration vest everything I'd need for a daily marathon.

I didn't yet know what would happen on day 18, or day 75, let alone day 100. There would still be plenty of challenges ahead, things that no amount of planning could truly prepare me for. But after doing what I could to set myself up for success, it was time to start running.

~

I can't remember the first time I saw the neat word trick I've come to view as the ultimate statement on self-doubt. Picture the word DOUBT, in capital letters, with the UBT scratched out to transform it into DO. Since I first encountered this image, I've returned to it over and over, putting it on the screen of my GPS watch and chalking it on the sidewalk so I can share it on social media. I even considered it as a title for this book!

You could say the message is to overcome your fears, so you can go about the business of doing what matters to you. And that is one way I read it. As writer and poet Suzy Kassem has said, "Doubt kills more dreams than failure ever will." It's all too easy to stand in your own way and let the possibility that you won't succeed prevent you from even considering something new and scary.

As my running journey continued, I came to see another meaning too: It's the doing itself that removes the doubt. Every single human has, from time to time, felt unsure of themselves. Those who are successful continue forging ahead despite those misgivings. And the more you *do*, the more confident you feel, ready to take the next big swing.

Now, every journey starts with one small step, or, if you're smart, a bit of planning and preparation. In the case of running, that means things like training your body, studying a course map, and getting the right gear. Long-distance runners quickly learn that there is an endless amount of data to obsess over, from pace to elevation charts to the number of grams of carbs you take in per hour. The longer the distance and the gnarlier the course, the more logistics you should consider.

You also have to know your own personality. I'm admittedly more of a go-with-the-flow runner, in part because I have no idea what my leg is going to do during any given run. My friend Jeannette, meanwhile, creates a detailed spreadsheet for every 100-miler—down to every aid station snack and change of socks—and she generally sticks to it. She freaks out a little bit every time I ask her to crew me during an ultramarathon, because I don't have a strict timeline laid out in advance.

But even if you're an uber-planner, if you're expecting all that groundwork to remove doubt and fear altogether, you'll be disappointed. You can never truly predict the outcome before you begin, and putting off a goal as you try to anticipate every what-if is another way of letting fear of the unknown win. At some point, you're going to get to the end of that particular diving board and make a jump into the deep end.

~

My first half marathon in Durham marked a significant turning point. After years of watching from the sidelines, it was my turn to be in on the action, part of something that both pushed me individually and tied me to a bigger community. No longer did I fear people seeing me in shorts; training in the summer heat in North Carolina demanded I wear them, and I didn't hesitate to do so. My focus had shifted from appearance to performance. I was all in on the sport, determined to find out just how much better I could be.

Each week, I'd head to the track workouts for intervals of fast running—painful but necessary to get better, I told myself. By June of 2017, I ran a 1-mile time trial in 7 minutes and 4 seconds. Not bad for someone who began at a pace slower than 11 minutes per mile! And after several more half marathons, I broke the 2-hour mark for that distance, running a time of 1:56:30 (that's 8 minutes, 53 seconds per mile) at the Tobacco Road Half Marathon in March of 2017.

Once you run half marathons, you start to figure you can do the full 26.2 miles. Many runners flock to the Abbott World Marathon Majors, a series of big-city races with a reputation for being well-organized and runner-friendly. I chose the Chicago Marathon because it's such a great city with a flat, fast course and a strong para-athletics program. The race was in October of 2017. I coordinated with the race organizers in the late spring, and before I knew it, I was officially in marathon training.

Any runner who's trained for their first marathon knows that, week by week, your long runs build. You might start with a distance you've done before, like 8 miles or 10 miles. Gradually, you add on, until every week becomes a journey into uncharted territory. Fourteen miles, 17 miles, 20 miles—each one presents a new test of your physical endurance and mental strength. However, you never actually get to the full race distance, 26.2 miles, during training. You have to trust that all the different elements of your training—those fast track workouts plus the slower, longer miles, and all the rest in between—will come together to carry you the distance.

As I built up, there were plenty of times I struggled to believe in myself. By August, I'd already completed a 17-mile long run. But one week, when I tried to run 18 miles, the 98 percent humidity dragged me down, and I had to stop after 13 miles. I now know that was a wise move—heatstroke is never beneficial for your fitness, after all!—and as I continued to gain more experience with running, I learned to let go of these less-than-perfect days.

But at the time, it made me feel like a failure, and the negative voices in my head started shouting. When I went to do my long run the next week, I came to a stop after 20 minutes. My brain had somehow just convinced me I wasn't cut out for this whole marathon-training thing after all. I didn't really see the point in continuing.

As soon as I stopped, I got even angrier at myself. I went home and vented to Edwin about what happened. "Take a step back," he said, "We all have bad runs. But you've come a long way, and you can keep going." He was right, I realized. I just needed to believe for a few steps more.

Once I'd calmed down, I went back outside and did another run, this time for 25 minutes. Then, a while later, I started again, running for 30 minutes. Each time, I coached myself through, out loud. "You've got this, Jacky," I'd say. I'm sure anyone who saw me wondered what in the heck I was going on about. But by the end of the day, I'd racked up 13.1 miles, not to mention a renewed sense of confidence. I was turning doubting into doing, a few miles at a time.

Running the marathon was both the hardest and most exhilarating thing I'd ever done to that point. The para-athletes actually start in the front, ahead of the elites. I was steps away from accomplished runners including Mo Farah and Brigid Kosgei, who'd go on to win, and top American runner Galen Rupp. We watched them warm up—noting their smooth, steady strides—and then, not long after we started, they whizzed past us.

I'd never been a part of a big-city race before, and the atmosphere was electric. We ran through twenty-nine different neighborhoods—past stages with bands, running-group cheer zones, and even lion dancers in costume in Chinatown. Spectators lined nearly every mile, ringing cowbells and shouting encouraging words. I always recommend this race to first-time marathoners. The looped course with a downtown start makes the logistics straightforward, and the course is free of hills save the tiny swell about 400 meters from the finish, on Roosevelt Road, affectionately known as Mount Roosevelt. Best of all, you truly can't beat the energy of the city on marathon day.

Edwin and I ran together, and until mile 20 we were moving at a steady clip. But not long afterward, I hit the notorious "wall" all runners dread, and everything fell apart. It's the moment when you run out of the glycogen that powers your muscles. Your legs begin to feel like lead, and your thoughts turn dark. I wanted to quit a million times, and by mile 25, I was so tired I could barely lift my legs. I was walking at the moment when I looked to the crowds and saw my friend Gregg. "Get to that finish line!" he yelled, helping me find a few ounces of energy I didn't know I still had in me.

I started running again, and as the Chicago crowds roared, we crossed the line. My time might not have been what I hoped, but I still qualified for the Boston Marathon by 47 minutes in my division.

Most importantly, less than a year and a half after I started my running journey, and after many moments of thinking it wasn't possible, I was now a marathoner.

~

For all my progress on the roads, I was also falling in love with the trails. There were plenty around us in Cary, and Edwin and I began venturing there together as he prepared for trail marathons and ultramarathons. The Loblolly Trail in Umstead State Park, a quick ten-minute drive from home, soon became my favorite. There's plenty of shade from loblolly pines and majestic white oaks, the trail is well maintained, and the soft dirt was a nice break from the impact of the roads and the track. The horseflies and the mosquitoes, now, I could do without, but if I kept moving, they didn't bother me so much, and they always liked Edwin better anyway.

About halfway through, a stream cuts over the path. The way across is a series of big, flat rocks with gaps at least a foot wide in between. The first time we reached it, I hesitated. My Catapult blade came with a rubbery tread affixed to the bottom, designed to protect the composite material and give me some traction. But it was made for the track and pavement—think more of a low-tread racing tire than a rugged all-terrain model. I was certain that if I took a wrong step with the blade, I'd slip and wind up face-first in the water.

I had a choice to make: Let fear hold me back, or try anyway.

Nervously, I inched across. It took me twenty minutes to reach the other side. Edwin waited patiently, ready to catch me if I fell, but otherwise letting me take my time. (He probably came away with a few extra bug bites that day, but he didn't complain too much.) When I got to the other bank, I paused to steady myself before running on.

Beyond the water, the trail was amazing, with serene views of a mossy lake. So after that first trail run, I went back again and again, each time with a bit more confidence, and also a replacement tread I'd fashioned by cutting out of the bottom of a pair of trail shoes and gluing the strip of rubber onto my blade. By the third time I crossed, I was skipping across the rocks in five minutes. Honestly, it felt just as satisfying—if not more so—than getting a new personal record in a race.

My gears started turning. Overcoming that first small barrier made me wonder what other problems I could solve. I had, at this point, seen other amputees out on the roads, but I'd never encountered any at one of Edwin's trail races. When I brought up the topic with others, the most common reaction I got was doubt and disbelief. Even the prosthetists I talked to told me amputees don't do trail running; there wasn't a foot made for that purpose, and they hadn't read about it in any of their books. I was likely to fall and break something, either my prosthetic or myself. I was better off staying on the flat, smooth road.

At this point, you can imagine my reaction. I immediately started Googling trail races.

After some searching, I settled on the Triple Lakes Trail Race through Bur-Mil Park in Greensboro, North Carolina, which would take place the following October. There was a half marathon, a marathon, and a 40-mile ultra. I could've chosen the half or the full, but, you know, I'd already covered those distances. I didn't overthink it; I just registered for the 40-miler.

The self-doubt began to kick in soon afterward. I coped by stalking social media, looking for others who'd completed the course. I reached out to a runner from Greensboro named Joe. He'd done it the year prior and written a thoughtful blog post about the experience. He wrote beautifully about all the ups and down: the other runners he connected with on the route, the leg cramps that sent him into the "pain cave" at mile 31, and the money he raised for Disabled American Veterans. I sensed a kindred soul, and while I acknowledged that it was probably strange for me to message him out of nowhere, I wanted to know more about what the course had in store for me.

He wrote back, graciously, and shared what he knew, from the climb in the first few meters to the tree roots that frequently trip up runners along the way. That Instagram exchange began a lovely friendship—and a well-timed one, because that was the year he became the Triple Lakes race director. About three weeks before the race, he invited me and Edwin to his home to meet him and his wife, Mary. She made us lunch while Joe took me out for a short 3-mile run on part of the course, helping me feel more comfortable with what I'd encounter there. All in all, it looked similar to what I'd been training on in Umstead, and that gave me confidence.

To continue preparing, I bought trail shoes for my right foot, worked my way up to longer distances in training, and made a plan for how I'd fuel my body for the duration, basing the number of sugary energy-boosting gels on what I'd used for the Chicago Marathon. The human body can store only a limited amount of glycogen—the fuel your muscles use to power every contraction—so the longer an athlete is out there, the more they need to top off their stores. Even as I made these calculations, though, I knew no one could tell me how my blade, or body, would hold up to a distance nearly twice as long as I'd gone before. I was equal parts excited and terrified, and ready to find out.

~

Four days before the race, I got an email from the race organizers. Hurricane Michael, which had swept from the Florida Panhandle upward the week prior, had made many of the trails in Bur-Mil Park unpassable. The race was still on, but instead of following a winding route from Lake Brandt and Lake Jeanette to Lake Townsend and back, we'd repeat the half-marathon course, circling Lake Brandt three times.

Okay, I thought, I guess it's now the Single Lake race rather than Triple Lakes! I was glad the event was at least still on, and I thought the course change might almost be easier. Rounding a single loop would break the mileage up in chunks, making the 40-mile distance feel less daunting. Plus, I'd be more familiar with the terrain on the second and third times around. Logistics were also easier for spectators. Usually there were twelve aid stations spread throughout the 40-mile course, and these made convenient rendezvous points that family and friends could drive to to check in on their athletes. They also featured tables stocked with supplies including gels, potatoes, bananas, and candy. (Most ultrarunners, I'd quickly learn, take in some solid foods in addition to gels. With longer efforts, your body needs more types of nutrients, and there's only so much sugar you can slurp down!) Now that the course had changed, there'd be just one aid station, near the start and finish of the loop. My family could stay in that spot, and I could see them each time I came around.

On race morning, it was a steamy 60°F. Edwin, the kids, the dog, and I all piled into the car and drove to the park. The vibe at the starting line was refreshingly low-key; compared to nearly 45,000 runners and 1.5 million spectators at the Chicago Marathon, this race had only about 200 participants across all the distances.

I looked down at my sparkling new trail shoe, purchased the week before, wondering what adventure lay ahead for us. The beautiful thing about a new race distance, especially when you're talking about trails, is that you don't feel the pressure of high expectations. I knew I wanted to finish, but other than that, I was open to what the day brought me.

It didn't take long to realize that the storm's effects on the trail didn't, in fact, make things easier. The first part of the course followed a paved bike path that was covered with mud, making it surprisingly slick. And then, once we entered the trail, the mud thickened, becoming a gloppy, squishy mess. I felt like I was running nearly sideways as I tried to navigate the path. With almost every step, my blade slipped, my poor road-ready tread no match for the slop. I shuffled, staring at my feet, trying my best not to slide or to bang my blade on the tough tree roots, which were now buried beneath the muck. I raised my head periodically only to check the flags that told me I was still on the course.

Now, I know I said I had no specific time goals or expectations…but this was so challenging, I almost had to laugh. My main goal had become to stay upright and to finish the race before the cutoff time. Nearly every race, even the smallest trail and ultra events, has a specific window in which you must complete the course. That's because when race organizers ask for permits, they have to list a start and end time, and volunteers need to know how long they'll be out there. Often, there are interim cutoffs at aid stations along the way to ensure you're on track to beat the overall course time limit. If you fall behind, you'll be stopped, and you won't receive an official finish time. (In runner terms, you'll get a DNF, or did not finish.)

Triple Lakes allowed 12 hours, or 18 minutes per mile, to reach the finish line. I thought, when I signed up, that this would be plenty of time. But as I slipped and slid, I was beginning to worry that my first trail ultra would end in a DNF.

About halfway through the loop, there was a series of small embankments, ramps that mountain bikers often leapt off as they rode the trails. I paused when I reached them. If I tried to run or walk down on my foot and my blade, I'd likely find myself on an unintentional Slip 'N Slide—fun for kids, but not so much for full-grown ultrarunners! I decided to sit and bum-shuffle my way down, chuckling a bit at how ridiculous I must look. But I made it to the bottom, got up, and kept going. When I saw Edwin and the kids after the first loop, I was still in good spirits, though my shoe was no longer so clean and sparkling.

Not long after, it began to sprinkle, making the terrain even more slick. And then, it happened. Around mile 16, my blade got stuck in a muddy spot, but the rest of me kept moving. My upper leg twisted around in my socket, and my whole body hit the ground. As I tumbled, my blade slammed into my right knee, crushing it.

For a moment, I sat on the soggy ground, assessing the situation. There were no other runners in sight. My knee pulsed with pain, the rain was growing steadier, and I had 24 miles to go. But I didn't dwell there long. Nothing was bloody or swollen, and when I stood up, I could put weight on my leg just fine. I aimed to put the struggles out of my mind and move ahead. I thought back to my conversations with Joe before the race. He'd also started running well into middle age and had quickly moved up in distance. He'd told me ultrarunning had shown him he was capable of anything. If he could make it through the pain cave we long-distance athletes so often encounter, I could too.

Those last nine miles were the longest of my life to that point, and among the loneliest. Earlier in the race, I'd watched other runners glide past me, and I'll admit there were times when I was a bit envious of the way they cruised over the roots and mud on their two legs. On road courses, I'd been rather competitive against runners without disabilities in my age group, and now here I was in the back of the pack, running by myself in the dark. My only company was the occasional bike that whooshed by, surprising and terrifying me, and the beady little eyes I sensed all around me. I'm not sure if they were spiders or rodents or some other type of critter, but I knew I wanted to get off the trail and away from them as fast as possible.

Fortunately, as I finally neared the finish line, I wasn't alone any longer. Every volunteer who'd been working the race that day—along with Edwin, the kids, and the dog—was there waiting for me. As they saw my headlamp approach, they all began to cheer, urging me on to the finish. I made it ahead of the cutoff, the last runner in, with minutes to spare.

I barely managed to hug Edwin and the kids before collapsing in a chair. I couldn't remember ever feeling so tired. My knee still ached, and my blade also needed a good wash. But despite finishing dead last, 28th out of 28, I smiled with gratitude for this welcoming community and the pride I felt in seeing just how far I'd gone outside my comfort zone. I had no clue what I was doing out there, but now that I'd had a taste of what it was like, I was already scheming about better ways to overcome the obstacles I'd encountered. I'd found my new home.

The next day, I could barely walk. Fortunately, I had no problem typing, and my credit card also worked just fine. So, of course, I signed up for a 50-miler.

4

JUST KEEP GOING

Marathons 1 Through 13 of 104

I finished my first 26.2 miles around the neighborhood in the early afternoon. I knew that if I was going to do this day after day, I'd have to pace myself. So I didn't rush this effort, and I finished in around 4 hours and 30 minutes.

January in Arizona is usually relatively mild, and this day was no exception. The temperature was right around 50°F when I started, and by midday it only reached 60°F, though the sun was bright overhead. When I returned home, I immediately reached for a recovery drink—a blend of carbs, protein, and electrolytes that replenished what I'd sweat out—before taking off my blade. I was pleased that my stump looked relatively unharmed, with no blistering or skin breakdown. I spent a few minutes icing it, hoping to keep it healthy and happy. Edwin poked his head out of his office to check in on me.

"How'd it go?" he asked.

"One down, ninety-nine to go," I said with a bit of a grin.

At that point, I was pretty darned hungry, so I raided the snack pantry. And then, when the kids got home from school at around 3:30, it was back to mom duty, helping with homework and signing permission slips, almost as if the marathon effort that day hadn't happened. After a family dinner, I squeezed in a few minutes of foam rolling before heading to bed on the early side. I slept fairly well that evening, knowing that tomorrow I'd be doing it all over again.

When I got up the next morning, my stump was a bit swollen. Once I got the kiddos off to school, it was time to head out again, but I slowed down even more, finishing day 2 in closer to five hours. *Forward is a pace*, I reminded myself. *This isn't about finishing times. Just keep moving.*

As the days passed, I continued to marvel at how well my body was adapting. I'd feel a bit tight at the start but then loosen up as I started running. I kept thinking, "Our bodies are amazing!"

That is, until day 11. Almost as soon as I started running, my right shin started to ache. I kept striding the streets around home, but the pain didn't let up.

It felt like shin splints—a pain that occurs when the fibrous tissue surrounding the shinbone, rich in nerves and blood vessels, becomes inflamed and irritated. It's common among new runners or those who ramp up their activity levels quickly. I supposed I checked that box. In the first week alone, I'd run 184 miles, far more than I'd ever logged before.

Not only that, I was spending a lot more of those miles than usual on hard concrete rather than on trails. The next day, I applied some KT tape to relieve pain, then took a break from pounding the roads and sidewalks and headed to the 1.6-mile loop around Veterans Oasis Park, less than a ten-minute drive away. I'd run in the park plenty before, and the groomed dirt trail felt cushiony beneath my blade. I parked in the lot, close to well-maintained bathrooms, and left lots of cool water and energy gels in my white Jeep, transforming it into a makeshift aid station. There were also vending machines where I could grab a backup snack or drink if I ran short on supplies.

I'd never seen a huge crowd there, but there were typically a few friendly birders, dogs and their humans, and other runners. I always had someone to smile and wave at as I rounded each bend, again and again and again.

I headed back there on day 12, my shin aching. That run turned into more of a shuffle, but I got it done. Still, I fretted. I knew shin splints could sometimes turn into stress fractures, small cracks in the bone that are exceedingly painful and, if you keep running on them, liable to turn into more serious medical issues. Could something so seemingly simple take me out so soon into the challenge? I hoped not.

That night, I iced my shin, used my massage gun, and applied some arnica gel, a homeopathic remedy for muscle pain and stiffness. The next day—marathon 13—I put on a compression sock, headed back to the soft trails, and tried again.

My shin felt so much better, I was shocked. My fear evaporated. I was going to be able to continue.

In the middle of my marathon that day, a man stopped me—a monk from Thailand, in full orange robes. At first, I thought maybe I was hallucinating. But he was real, and he exuded positive energy. He'd never seen a leg like mine and was full of questions about how I could run on it.

"How far are you going?" he asked me.

"Twenty-six point two miles today, and then tomorrow, and every day for eighty-six days after that," I said.

"How," he said, clearly shocked, "is that even possible?"

I thought a moment before answering. "One step at a time," I said.

~

Learning to run was a process, as I've explained. But long before I could do that, I had to learn to walk again.

After my amputation, my doctors wanted me to start down the road toward getting a prosthetic as quickly as possible. The sooner I could begin walking on a new leg, the easier it would be for my brain and body to adapt. They took the first cast—placing plaster around my stump to begin shaping a temporary socket—when I was still in the hospital.

A couple of weeks later, I received my first, temporary prosthetic leg. My incision was healing, but my stump was still raw and sensitive. When a limb is removed, the tissue needs time to repair, and the nerves need some time to adjust, now that they no longer connect to the places they used to go. Sometimes they keep firing, and the brain interprets those signals as pain or phantom sensations. Nerves can even clump together in a tight bundle to create an excruciating growth called a neuroma.

The stump is also swollen by the inflammation the immune system uses to heal the wound. Think about how much a relatively minor injury like an ankle sprain puffs up, and you can imagine how fiercely the body responds when repairing damage from something as severe as amputation. It can take time—a year or two, even—for the stump to shrink to its final shape. Remember that the socket that holds the prosthetic on is specially designed for each person and needs to fit snugly and properly; during the early stages, it's common to need to replace it frequently as the swelling goes down bit by bit. Navigating all this requires equal parts perseverance and patience.

I was in the middle of this process when I went back to work, just four weeks after my surgery. I was using my prosthetic, though I still had crutches too. There's a lot about that time that's a blur to me, but I remember that my early steps on the new leg were overwhelming, physically and mentally. The pressure irritated my raw nerve endings and triggered the phantom pain I was already coping with—that bizarre crossed-toes feeling I had no idea how to relieve. And while sometimes I would feel fine for a while, there would, all of a sudden, be a shock of pain so severe it took my breath away and made me want to rip off the prosthetic.

Then there was the mental piece. My brain simply didn't view the new limb as a part of me. When I first placed it down to take a step, it was nearly impossible to put my full weight onto it; that's why new amputees usually walk first between parallel bars and on crutches. It wasn't just the pain, although it did hurt. More significant was my lack of trust in the idea that this foreign object could prevent me from crashing to the floor.

At the time, back in 2002, there was no social media and no large online community of amputees to share experiences with and gain knowledge from. My doctors and therapists explained the nuts and bolts, but they couldn't explain how I should be feeling inside. With so many new and strange sensations, I couldn't tell what was normal for the healing process and what was a sign I had pushed too hard or needed a tweak to my socket. The only way to learn and build confidence was to keep trying.

So I pushed on, taking a few more steps each day. Some days, I'd overdo it and have to rest more or lean more heavily on the crutches the next. But other times, I realized I could go farther than I thought. I began to notice which sensations were a sign that I'd pushed it just a bit too far and needed to back off, and which discomfort I could push through without making it worse.

Gradually, I also started to learn which type of pain came from my socket not fitting properly. It's hard to explain, but for me, it sort of feels like a bad bruise that doesn't go away. Part of why this happens in my case is because of the way my surgery was performed. At the time, the thinking was that leaving more of my fibula intact would improve my balance. But that also left my stump long and narrow, without much meat or padding on the bottom, and this means I'm highly prone to negative sensations due to rubbing and pressure.

The bottom line is that each person is unique. Others with amputations may have had their surgeries performed differently. Some people also lose limbs due to trauma, and their tissue may be damaged in ways that change how their prosthetics fit and feel. I always tell new amputees to speak up if something doesn't feel right. It's your prosthetist's job to make your limb as comfortable as possible, but they can't know what's going on inside your body. You need a thorough, nuanced conversation—an ongoing dialogue between you, your stump, and your healthcare team—to learn to decode the signals your body is sending you.

Now, decades later, I'm much better at telling the difference between normal aches, irritation from an ill-fitting socket, and pain that signals a brewing injury. What's more, my motor cortex has remapped to accept the new leg as part of me. In the weeks and months after my surgery, whenever I woke up and moved to get out of bed, I would automatically extend my missing leg toward the floor before remembering it was gone. Now, I reflexively reach to put on my prosthetic before I get up. The sheer fact that I just kept going, day after day, changed my brain so once-inconceivable tasks soon became second nature and ever-more-dramatic challenges eventually felt within reach.

~

What I didn't fully appreciate until I started running was just how much all this trial and error would benefit me as an athlete. Yes, there was an entirely new learning curve to running on a blade, and then still more to understand and absorb once I transitioned to trails. But these two abilities—to keep moving despite some types of pain and discomfort, while also knowing when it's wiser to change direction or take a pause—are the keys to a successful running career.

I've already shared one of my favorite mantras: "You can do hard things." Another is "You're capable of more than you think." But one mantra that doesn't particularly resonate with me is "No pain, no gain." Running isn't a way to punish myself but a source of freedom and joy. And there are many times when continuing to train or race despite fatigue, illness, or a minor niggle can actually backfire and turn into burnout or major injury.

You don't always know where that line is before you cross it. But I believe it's wisest to have grace for yourself rather than beating yourself up if you *do* get hurt or dig yourself into a hole. I also don't believe in glorifying suffering for its own sake.

Sometimes, when my stump is swollen or bruised or I'm mentally exhausted, I opt for a long walk instead of pushing myself through a run that might break me. My calculation also considers my long-term priorities and what's next on my calendar. I'm far more likely to test the outer limits of what I can endure during an event I've been dreaming of for months than on a training run or tune-up race leading up to it.

But experience has taught me that many types of pain and struggle aren't, in fact, insurmountable. When I run with a prosthetic, there's rarely a time when I feel zero discomfort. As I train, I learn to make adjustments that bring as much relief as possible, and then to make peace with any pain that remains. In the end, my proudest moments often come from continuing when I want to stop.

April 2019

After the Triple Lakes 40-miler, I knew I wanted more—and longer—adventures on the trails. The park where I did much of my training, Umstead, had a 50- and 100-mile race in the spring. So the next spring, I signed up for the 50-miler while Edwin took on the 100, his first attempt at a triple-digit distance.

This time, I'd be better equipped than I had on that muddy Triple Lakes race. My first order of business was to purchase some poles. When I started running trails, I didn't know other runners used them; I considered them a sign of weakness at best, cheating at worst. But the more I immersed myself in the running community, the more I realized how many people brought them onto more technical courses. I tried them out and quickly noted they offered better traction, stability, and speed—helpful for any runner, but particularly crucial for me as someone who had the extra balance challenge of a prosthetic.

I also started exploring whether there were other, better blades for rough terrain. My Catapult foot wasn't as responsive as I would've liked, and even outside of the fall I'd taken, it caused other problems I wanted to avoid. Each time I hit a rock, it twisted in the opposite direction of my stump, rather than moving with the rest of my body. The feeling was something like constantly tweaking an ankle. "This is something I can fix," I thought. Every ultrarunner spends some time in the pain cave, but I wanted that feeling to come from the enormity of my effort, not a mismatch between my equipment and my environment. If there were better tools for my adventures, it made sense to find them.

Now, there isn't a catalog of prosthetics for trail ultrarunners—we're a small population, after all! I didn't know if there was anyone else doing as much mileage as me, especially on the same tough courses. But now that I'd proven trail running was within the realm of possibility for me, and now that I had an idea of what it required, my prosthetist Chandler and I began brainstorming together.

Some legs had more rugged treads, which might provide better traction, but they were also heavier than I liked. I was intrigued, though, when he brought up the Fillauer Obsidian. It was slightly heavier than my existing blade, but still lighter than some of the other options. Most importantly, it had a split toe, which offered more responsiveness to the ground. I still wouldn't be able to flex my calf, swivel my ankle, or sense a rock underfoot, but when I tried it out in his office, I could see how, if I hit a rock on one side of the blade, the toes would separate slightly rather than twisting my entire leg in the opposite direction of my stump. I couldn't wait to take it for a whirl on the trail.

~

My new blade hadn't yet arrived in time for my Umstead 50-miler, but I still showed up far more prepared than I had for Triple Lakes.

With Edwin's help, I'd glued an even sturdier tread onto the bottom of my Catapult. I ran as many hills as I could in training to build strength for the more than 3,500 feet of climbing I'd do over four laps of the 12.5-mile course.

Add some better trail shoes and the poles, subtract the hurricane and mud, and perhaps it's no surprise that I hit the 40-mile mark two hours faster than I had at Triple Lakes, then went on to run 10 miles more. Things got tough in the last loop, with my blade causing some friction on my stump, but I don't think I stopped smiling for the entire 12 hours and 13 minutes.

In the weeks afterward, my new blade came in and I started putting it to the test. Immediately, I could tell it was going to be a game-changer on the trails. It was bouncier and moved with my body more smoothly, as if I were gliding over rather than bumping against every rock and root. And from the beginning, I was doing things I never thought imaginable—literally hopping up and down on it, doing box jumps onto a bench, and practicing single-leg deadlifts.

If you'd shown me videos of those movements when I first started walking on a prosthetic, or even running on one, I don't think I would've believed they were real. But my confidence was rising, and each repetition further strengthened the trust and connection between my mind, muscles, and blade. Plus, I needed all the strength and stability I could get. I was about to take on my toughest test yet: the TransRockies three-day stage race.

Following my ever-expanding sense of adventure, I'd signed up for a competition to earn a slot for this race from Hyland's, a company that makes natural medicines and supplements. After an interview, they'd selected me for their team for this event, and I couldn't have been more excited. I'd be joining accomplished ultrarunner Mirna Valerio and receiving guidance from her coach, Mike Ehredt.

Mirna was a true inspiration. Like me, she was a later bloomer. Though she'd run in high school, she spent years away from the sport before a health scare brought her back in 2018. She also didn't fit the typical mold of a trail ultrarunner; as a Black woman in a larger body, she frequently deals with doubters and naysayers too. Still, she continues to share her story so that others who see themselves in her journey can draw hope from it.

In August, I'd head to Buena Vista, Colorado, where the race would begin at 8,000 feet above sea level. Over three days, we'd travel 60 miles along a mix of trails, four-wheel-drive routes, and forest service roads in the Rocky Mountains, gaining another 8,000 feet of vert along the way. At night, we'd camp together and talk about the day's adventures.

Nothing I could do in North Carolina could prepare me for the altitude—we lived at 384 feet—so I simply had to hope that running through the heat and humidity of a Southern summer would build up enough red blood cells to help me perform in an environment with less oxygen. But I *could* practice climbing. I alternated between the hilliest trails I could find and the treadmill, cranking the incline up to 12 percent. To mimic the back-to-back efforts, I'd run two 2-hour sessions on it, morning and night. I also added in stair repeats—calculating that 1 mile equaled about 52 floors of climbing, or 500 feet of elevation gain. At first, I had to hold onto the handrails, especially down the stairs. Eventually, I learned to place my blade on the front of the steps on the descent so I wouldn't tip over the edge.

By the time August rolled around, I was as ready as I could be.

I arrived in Colorado on August 11 and was thrilled to finally meet Mirna and Mike in real life. Mirna was as lovely in person as she is online, and we fell into an easy conversation, chatting about everything from our race experiences to our children. Her son, Rashid, is an athlete as well—a tall and talented basketball player. She beamed whenever she mentioned him.

Tuesday morning, August 13, we lined up at the start in front of the Surf Hotel & Chateau in beautiful Buena Vista. The sun was brutally hot for all 22 miles, but at least that stage featured the least amount of climbing. I was happy with how my blade held up as we traveled across surfaces that shifted from gravel and rock to sand, but at the end of the day, I was wiped from the heat, and my stump was covered in blisters. I'd never had them so bad and wasn't sure how to treat them, but as we gathered at camp that evening, the medical staff checked to make sure they were clean and in good enough condition that I could return to the starting line the next morning.

The next day, August 14, was my birthday. After a decent night's sleep in the tent and breakfast at camp, we boarded school buses to Vicksburg, Colorado, a ghost town near the turnaround of the famous Leadville Trail 100 Run. We started with a steep climb up to Hope Pass, which sits at an altitude of 12,500 feet. Leadville runners take this path twice, but I have to say that once was grueling enough! My new poles got plenty of use as I made my way to the top along the rocky single-track trail.

As usual, I stared down at my feet most of the time; since I can't feel the ground beneath me, I need to be sure where I'm placing each step. But every once in a while, I'd glance up through the tall aspen forests or marvel at the peaks revealing themselves in the distance. It was truly an incredible sight. It's tough to know whether it was from the natural beauty, the thin air, or the steep terrain, but I frequently found myself breathless.

For most of the day, I ran near two fantastic runners. Doug Malewicki is an engineer and inventor who spent his life developing new transit systems and, at eighty years old, was still crushing it on the trails. He was part of a two-person team, called the California Old Goats, with Gordy Ainsleigh, seventy-five at the time and a literal trailblazer of ultrarunning. Each day, when they finished the stage, they'd stand near the finish line with business cards to hand to the runners behind them that said, "You've been geezered."

But no one should've been embarrassed to fall behind such formidable athletes. In the 1970s, Gordy rode his horse several times in the Tevis Cup, a 100-mile endurance trail ride in the Sierra Nevada range, and at times, he'd hop off to jog alongside his mount. But in 1974, his horse went lame, so Gordy decided to do the entire distance on foot—the only human among 250 horses.

The temperature was 107°F the day of Gordy's race. The aid stations had only hay, grain, and water. Fueling-wise, he was stuck with only a couple of packets of electrolytes in his pockets, a can of peaches he'd swiped from race organizers, and some Gatorade he'd stashed on the course beforehand. There were times he wanted to stop. But he never did like quitting, and none of the veterinarians at the health check stations he passed told him he was in danger, so he persisted. He finished in 23 hours and 42 minutes—within the cutoff time, and even passing several horses along the way. In the following years, enough other runners wanted to repeat his feat that a separate event along the same course—the Western States Endurance Run—was born. It's now the most prestigious 100-miler, sometimes called the Super Bowl of ultrarunning.

I couldn't believe I was there alongside ultrarunning royalty, and I found Gordy to be incredibly intellectual, not to mention well-traveled. As we ran, we discussed our adventures all over the world. He was curious to know more about my time growing up in South Africa, and he shared stories of his far-flung runs. When we got to the top of Hope Pass, I made sure we paused for a photo together. The vista was stunning and made all the effort more than worth it.

But what goes up must come down, and the route from Hope Pass to Twin Lakes is steep and technical. The first section had snow, and my blade had zero traction. So I did what I'd learned during Triple Lakes and bum-shuffled my way down.

Once we were back on the rocky trail, I was chatting with the woman in front of me and Gordy behind me. We were just about at the 8-mile mark of the 13 miles we'd cover that day when we reached a switchback. I'm not sure what happened—my blade may have hit a root or a rock—but one second I was upright and the next I was airborne.

Everything moved in slow motion. I could see the ground approaching, and I thought to myself, "This is gonna hurt." Then,

I slammed down hard against the dirt trail, hitting my knee first before the rest of my body followed. Gordy and the other runners around me gasped audibly and stopped. I laid there on my side for a moment, then they helped me onto my back.

I wasn't sure what would happen next. The others seemed skeptical that I could continue. Even Gordy—who also happens to be a chiropractor—told me my knee looked pretty bad.

Perhaps it was the adrenaline or the thought of Gordy chasing horses in the heat, but once my fellow runners helped me to my feet, I chose to keep moving. My hip and knee both ached, but nothing—including my blade—seemed broken. I may well have torn something; to this day I still have a dent on my thigh from that fall. But out there in the mountains, I found I had what I needed within me to continue.

When I reached the finish line, limping and in tears—I swear I do these things for fun!—I could hardly believe what I saw. Edwin, Dexter, and Eliza had flown out from North Carolina to surprise me. My kids held a banner that said "Happy Birthday"; my sniffles turned into a full-blown ugly cry as my emotions overwhelmed me. Happy, hurting, tough, fortunate, fragile—add it all up and I'd never felt more *alive*.

That night, instead of staying in camp, I went with Edwin and the kids to their hotel. I could barely walk. Everyone, Edwin included, assumed I wouldn't be back to finish the next stage. I wasn't sure either, but honestly, I wasn't thinking that far ahead. I took a bath, which eased some of the tightness and soreness, and crashed into bed.

The next morning, I slowly and cautiously opened my eyes. I did a mental scan of my body before moving. "Hmmm," I thought, "not nearly as awful as I'd expect." In fact, I felt perfectly fine. I put on my leg, got up, and announced that I wanted to go to Leadville for the race start. Could Edwin drive me? He looked at me, stunned.

"Who are you?" he asked. "You can't be the same person who fell yesterday." But once he got over his shock, he knew better than to doubt me.

We left in a hurry and made it just in time for the mandatory safety inspection. At the start of stages 2 and 3, due to the elevation changes and unpredictable weather, the race directors require each runner to have a warm beanie, light gloves, a jacket, and an emergency blanket. To my horror, I realized that, in my haste, I'd forgotten nearly all my gear! Fortunately, a kind couple who'd driven their camper van to the start had an extra set of all the supplies I needed. The community came to my rescue, and I was off for the last 25 miles of my first 60-miler.

In the days after I finished, I couldn't stop looking at the pictures from the race. Long gone was the woman who'd covered her prosthetic with long pants and avoided mirrors. Here I was, in shorts and sunglasses, raising my running poles into the air as the beauty of the Rocky Mountains glowed behind me. The distance I'd traveled, I realized, couldn't be measured in merely miles or meters of vert.

We all face situations outside our control, challenges we didn't choose. And setting a goal and doing the work isn't a guarantee we'll reach the finish. In fact, many times, I've had to change plans before I even reached the starting line—such as the time when, in the days before one mountain race, I banged my ankle on a hotel room bed and couldn't even start.

External factors like cutoff times can also lead to a change in plans. If I'm hurting and it slows my pace so much I'm told I can't continue, I know I'll just have to come back to try again another day.

But each time I fall and get back up, each time I think I can't continue and I do it anyway, something in my mind and body shifts. Just as my brain rewired itself to run with a prosthetic, persistence connects the mental muscle that powers my resilience. People often ask me how I can keep going when things get tough. Sometimes I feel like *I'm* the monk when I answer, "I just keep going."

5

CELEBRATE SMALL WINS

Marathon 18 of 104

In the classic nineties movie *Groundhog Day*, a grumpy weatherman played by Bill Murray finds himself living the same day over and over. It happens to be February 2, when all eyes turn to Punxsutawney Phil and his prediction about the end of winter.

Well, Groundhog Day—February 2—was day 18 of my marathon record attempt. With just over 470 miles down and 2,000-plus to go, I resonated with Murray's character, feeling more than a touch of déjà vu. Just as I did nearly every day, I packed the kids off to school, then headed out to run for several hours.

With the ultimate finish line so far in the future, there were plenty of times my mind played tricks on me, convincing me it was fine to quit even when what I most wanted was to continue. Grinding through the low moments required breaking my one massive goal into much more modest milestones.

At the end of that day's marathon, like most of the others, I acknowledged my accomplishment to myself and my social media followers. I saved a template on my computer, updated it with my new total of marathons run and those left to complete, and printed out a copy. I held it up, had Edwin take a photo of me, and then posted it for my community to see. The likes and encouraging comments I got provided an added hit of motivating dopamine.

I also had benchmarks that were even more bite-sized. On tough days, when I reached each mile or even half-mile mark, I would literally cheer out loud. I'm sure anyone watching thought I was a bit batty! If I started again after stopping for a breath or a water break, I offered myself heartfelt congratulations. And I applied the same approach to tackling the other responsibilities of life too. In the evening, if I successfully made family dinner or tossed in a load of laundry, I practically threw a party. These moments of recognition get me through the moment and make the whole journey feel more manageable, even joyous.

~

There's nothing like the feeling of finishing a race and having a volunteer place a big, shiny medal around your neck—or, in the case of some ultramarathons, hand you a belt buckle. It's true that, when Edwin started running, I questioned whether those tiny pieces of metal were truly worth all the sweat and effort he put in.

However, now I know how incredibly special that bling becomes when you've earned it. Plus, I have to say, race awards are a lot bigger and flashier now than they were a decade ago, especially here in the United States!

But I've also come to learn something else about medals and other awards, and it's that they aren't enough, by themselves, to keep you going. If you're going to train for months, then take on a race or another challenge that lasts hours (or, you know, 100-plus days!), you simply have to set smaller goals along the way. And you must truly revel when you reach them.

It might seem unimportant, or even self-defeating, to cheer for each mile when your goal involves 2,620 of them. But behavior-change experts have found that celebrating small wins doesn't take away from your bigger accomplishments, it actually *increases* the odds you'll reach your long-term aims. What's more, it keeps you happier, motivated, and clear on your purpose along the way.

When I first started running, the small goals were mostly about numbers—a personal record in the mile or a 5K, a higher placement in my age group, more feet of elevation climbed or miles covered in a day, week, month, or year. There's nothing wrong with that, and when you're new to running, the swift progress you can make in all these areas is downright addictive. I won't lie, I still measure a lot, and I take pride in hitting certain stats.

But especially as you mature in the sport, it's also important to have goals or landmarks that honor the fact that progress isn't always linear and running is about making your life fuller, not reducing it to a set of statistics. If I'm sore or injured, I celebrate making the choice to rest—and when I return, I rejoice at my first pain-free mile. Sometimes, a small win can be as simple as tying your shoes that morning, foam rolling that night, or stopping during your run to appreciate the view. Victories can also come in the form of a smile and a wave from a fellow athlete, or a deep, heartfelt conversation that lasts miles, or the support you get from your team in moments of struggle.

November 2021

Drive west of Phoenix into the Sonoran Desert, and a stark white building rises out of the sand—a gorgeous Victorian mansion called Nardini Manor. Usually, the one-hundred-year-old home and five-acre plot host weddings and upscale luncheons, with white folding chairs, floral arches, and guests dressed to the nines. But on this day, the gravel loop that winds around its grounds was filled with runners pushing the outer limits of possibility at the Fat Ox Endurance Runs.

See, in addition to hosting fancy receptions, Nardini Manor has a 500-meter running track that's certified by USA Track & Field (so you know it's accurately measured). It's home to a whole series of races organized by Aravaipa Running, a trail and endurance company. Check out Nardini Manor's Instagram page and you'll see a funny mix of glamorous brides and champagne flutes alongside sweaty athletes toting water bottles.

Unlike a 26.2-mile marathon or a 100-mile ultramarathon, the events held here are not distance-based but time-based. That means that over a given duration—in the case of Fat Ox, it's 12 hours, 24 hours, or 48 hours—each participant runs as much as they can manage, taking pit stops and refreshment breaks as needed, until their time is up. I'd chosen the middle option, aiming to see how far I could get in one day.

Within that big goal, it's always smart to set smaller mid-race objectives, such as maintaining a steady clip, covering a set number of loops or miles per hour, or limiting rest time. I didn't have hard-and-fast numbers in mind, but I aimed to keep my forward momentum as long as possible.

The vibe at these types of races tends to be welcoming and friendly. They draw a crowd of runners looking to do things their way and get the best out of themselves, rather than simply move from point A to point B as quickly as possible. Many are older—like my friend Teresa, who's nearly twenty years my senior and has been running ultras since the early 2000s. It's a great fit for certain kinds of runners; after all, the format rewards endurance, ingenuity, and perseverance rather than speed.

Next to the course, by the start and finish line, there was a huge lawn where runners and spectators could set up chairs, sleeping bags, or anything else they needed to get through the hours and days. The nearby aid station rotated its offerings based on the time of day—pancakes for breakfast, sandwiches for lunch, burgers for dinner, and a wide range of snacks in between. Yes, ultras can sometimes feel like eating contests and social gatherings in addition to athletic events! But don't be fooled: there's still a *lot* of running involved.

And despite the festive atmosphere, by 10 miles in—that's 32 laps of the less-than-half-mile loop—I was already feeling sore and weary. For reasons I hadn't quite pinpointed, my stump was extra sensitive, and as the discomfort altered my gait, I felt it causing tightness in my hip flexors. I was also annoyed by a particular quirk of this race, which is that every 3 hours, the organizers had us switch directions, finishing our lap around an orange cone and then heading back to run the loop the other way. You might think this would be a welcome change-up, but I always find it an interruption to my rhythm, and on this day the maneuver further irritated my stump.

I could tell the pain wasn't anything that would cause permanent damage, and so I chose to push ahead. "Forward is forward," I told myself, as always.

What this race lacks in novel scenery, it makes up for in built-in benchmarks. The mansion is guarded by a pair of lions, with a gazebo on the side and a hedge maze near the back of the property. Each time around, clocking those features felt like a mental check-mark. So, too, did seeing Edwin, who'd come to support me. When I needed a snack, a few words of encouragement, or even company for a lap, I could count on him—at least for the first 12 hours, from 8:00 a.m. to 8:00 p.m. At that point, he headed home to get a bit of rest before coming back with the kids to watch me finish.

When he left, I was in twentieth place overall and ninth female. I knew because there's a giant screen, like a scoreboard, just past the timing mat that serves as the start and finish line. I still wasn't feeling great, and at sometime around 1:00 a.m., I texted Edwin to tell him I was probably going to quit when I hit the 40-mile mark.

When I saw my watch turn over from 39.99, I stopped, rested my feet in my chair, and took in a bit of fuel. As I gazed around, I noticed that most of the other runners had halted their progress too. Some of them were even napping. I'm not sure if it was the calories or a burst of competitive spirit, but something about the scene inspired me to step back onto the track and keep going. Gazebo, lions, maze. Gazebo, lions, maze. I rounded the dirt track, again and again and again.

Edwin texted me back at around 3:00 a.m. He'd woken up, looked at the race tracker, and was shocked to see I was still going. "Holy sh$t, you are fourth woman and ninth overall!" he wrote. Teresa was one spot ahead of me, and as night turned to morning, the possibility of catching her kept me fired up to continue. That, by the way, is proof that your motivation can definitely change over time—and not just throughout a running career or a training cycle but even within the same race!

I couldn't quite reach her, but as the clock struck 8:00 a.m. and I finished my final lap, I was still trying. In the end, I stayed fourth female and eighth overall, finishing a total of 71.1 miles in 24 hours. That's 229 laps and 159,376 steps, my Garmin GPS watch told me—a lot of mini milestones, to be sure.

The reward for this race wasn't a medal or a buckle but a very cool wooden finisher's coaster. In the middle, the ox from the race's logo lifts its hoof in victory. I put it in a display cabinet in my living room. Each time I pass by, I'm reminded that I'm much stronger than I think.

June 2003

I prefer long distances. I'm terrified of heights. And my blade isn't great in the snow.

But for some reason, a year and a half after the Fat Ox, I found myself running straight up a ski mountain for 3 miles, on a course so snowy they delayed the start to cut more steps into the drifts for athletes to climb up.

Sponsors of the Broken Arrow Skyrace—a three-day, eight-distance sky racing event at Palisades Tahoe, a ski resort in California—had originally offered me a spot to run the 11K distance there, an up-and-down loop with more than 2,000 feet each of gain and loss. The race draws top runners across many disciplines, from champion mountain racers to athletes who run Olympic trials qualifying times on the track. I was honored to be there, and to be invited to speak on a nutrition panel too. It was yet another chance to step outside my comfort zone, considering I'm not the best at downhill running and get nervous about presenting in public. For all the progress I've made at staying balanced on my blade, I'm still scared of falling on descents, so I find myself being a bit cautious, braking and slowing more than I'd like.

That year, the area had its snowiest season on record, including a total of 191 inches of snow in March. Uncharacteristically, they even kept the ski slopes open until July 4! As much as I embrace each new adventure, there are some truths I just can't avoid, and one of those is that I'm never going to be a great snow runner. Eleven kilometers, or 7 miles, felt like way too much given the slipperiness of the slopes, and so I decided to leave that to the winter athletes. Instead, I switched to a race called the VK or vertical kilometer (since renamed the Ascent).

The course varies a little each year, but in 2023, it was 4.8 kilometers, or just under 3 miles. It began at the Olympic Village, in a valley of the Sierra Nevada, and ascended two peaks. First, we'd climb the iconic KT-22 summit, home to one of the country's most famous chairlifts. Then we'd scale Washeshu Peak, a flat-top mountain nearly 8,900 feet into the clouds.

As I studied the course beforehand, I went back and forth about which equipment to use. Some of the race emails suggested wearing spikes, or shoes with thick lugs to provide better traction on ice and snow. I considered the possibility of gluing spikes onto my blade, but then I remembered that I'd likely be power hiking most of this extreme course rather than running. So I decided to choose my walking leg, which allowed me to wear two shoes.

Race morning, I lined up beside 450 other athletes. The vibe was positive and inviting, with runners of all ages and even a few dogs around. (I didn't spot any other amputees.) Before we began, race director Brendan Madigan lifted his bullhorn and told us we were rock stars whether we finished first or last. He even invited us to give the runners to our right and left huge hugs before we began. And then everyone started heading directly uphill.

The first climb was brutal—half of the race's total 3,000 feet of ascent came in the first mile. And did I mention the slippery footing? I'd chosen trail shoes that were grippy but not full-on spikes. That was a mistake. I slowly, step by step and with the help of my trusty poles, climbed my way up toward KT-22. Before I knew what was happening, I was sliding back down the snowbank.

"Well," I thought as I skidded to a stop near the bottom, "this isn't great." But as you're no doubt starting to understand by now, obstacles are a part of the game in trail running. So I tried again—and once again, I slipped right back down to where I started from. A third attempt produced the exact same result.

At that point, if I'd been wearing a mic, it would've picked up a swear word or two. I was about to give up and let myself slide all the way down to meet Edwin in the valley. But then, seemingly out of nowhere, a kind volunteer appeared and started walking behind me, encouraging me along. The fourth time, in this case, was a charm. I pushed my way up, trying my best to get traction by stepping into the tracks left by others, and kept going.

Once I finally reached the top of KT-22, I had to navigate about a half mile of icy downhill before starting the final climb to Washeshu Peak. You'd better believe there was some bum-shuffling involved! And then, after a bit of climbing on a fire road, as I finally neared the finish, I hit the most terrifying moment of all.

In the rockiest section, there's a fairly sketchy-looking iron ladder soldered directly into the side of Washeshu Peak. Yes, there's a rope running alongside it that you can hang on to, but precious little else separates you from a tumble down the side of the mountain. And if you fall, you're done for. "Perhaps," I thought, "that's why they call this feature the Stairway to Heaven."

Now, I knew this was part of the course when I signed on. Still, when I saw exactly how narrow and exposed it was, tears brimmed in my eyes—tears that were quickly blown away by 50-mile-an-hour wind gusts. "What made you think this was a good idea, Jacky?" I asked myself. "You can't do this." But there wasn't any other way except up, as heading back down the way I'd come wasn't any less petrifying. I steeled myself and took one cautious step at a time—twenty or so more tiny victories over doubt and fear.

From there, I just had to ascend one more set of ice steps to reach the finish line. "If I slip here," I thought, "it's another quick ticket to heaven." But I didn't, and, finally, Broken Arrow's famous bell rang for me as I reached the flags that marked the finish line.

Those 3 miles took me nearly 3 hours. Though I wasn't quite dead last, I was close. I certainly wasn't clamoring to sign up for another sky race after that, and yet standing on the top of Washeshu Peak with my medal, I was enormously proud of what it took to get there. Even better: Another volunteer, noticing my fatigue, saved me the stress of bum-shuffling the snowy mile or so back down to the gondola that would take me to the valley. "Here," he said kindly, "I drove this snowmobile up here, and I have to take these supplies back down. Hop on and I'll take you too." His driving was almost as fearsome as my original slide down the slopes, to be honest. Still, I couldn't have asked for a better way to cap off the day than to hitch a (very fast) ride with a new friend.

~

Most races have a clear end point, whether it's a time or a distance or a point at the top of a mountain. But life isn't always like that; you might not even be sure where the finish line of a particular challenge or goal is, let alone how long it will take to reach it. When I got my cancer diagnosis, I had no clue what life would look like afterward. As tough as it was to see anything positive during that time, I learned it was far easier to cope if I truly celebrated each encouraging test result, decrease in pain level, or step toward walking on a prosthetic.

Even as I reached toward a new normal physically, I was far from the finish line psychologically. I'll be blunt: Amputation is hell on your body image. Long before my cancer diagnosis, I was prone to negative thoughts about my appearance. As a teenager, convinced I needed to be as thin as the models I saw in magazines, I developed an eating disorder. I received treatment and recovered, but as most people who have coped with conditions like anorexia will tell you, those thoughts linger in the back of your mind long after you leave therapy. So perhaps it's no surprise that, when I learned I'd be losing my leg, my mind immediately jumped to how disfigured and ugly I'd be. It feels strange to say now, because I know my worth isn't related to my appearance.

For years, I stuffed my prosthetic, and my feelings, into long pants. But I couldn't do that indefinitely, and there were times when everything would bubble to the surface again anyway.

My pregnancies, for example, tried my spirit. As happy as I was to grow my family, I struggled with the changing shape of my body. I steered even farther away from mirrors and cameras; I don't know if I have a single photo of myself from those times. At my so-called advanced maternal age—I was thirty-five when I got pregnant with Dexter in 2009 and thirty-seven with Eliza—I had to undergo lots of extra testing, and all that poking and prodding made things even more uncomfortable.

Weight gain also changed the shape of my stump and added pressure to my prosthetic, making it more difficult to walk. There wasn't much point in making adjustments, since everything would change again after each baby was born, and so instead I just became much more sedentary, which didn't help my mood.

I adore being a mom, and as my kids grew older, I began to have more appreciation for the body that brought them here. But still, I hid my differences. I sweltered in long pants on the hottest summer days. When we went to the beach or the pool, I was the person sitting fully dressed on a towel, watching my family splash and play without me. I hung back, in the shade, like a shadow.

Running changed all of that, one sweaty mile at a time.

I can't remember the first day I pulled on a pair of shorts instead of pants or even capris. But gradually, without realizing it, a series of small moments added up to a new way of being.

As I continued falling in love with the sport, I posted pictures of myself running on social media, for the whole world to see. At first, I fretted that I didn't look like a "real runner." The more I accomplished, though, the less I fell victim to that mindset. Once you've run marathons, ultramarathons, and intense mountain races, your imperfect body starts to feel downright amazing.

During my very first 5K, in 2016, I'd felt too exposed and naked to take off my painful walking leg without Edwin shielding me. Now, I switch between my walking and my running legs at aid stations or sitting in the back of my pickup truck before trail runs. I no longer care who sees my stump as I smear Squirrel's Nut Butter salve on it to ease chafing, then pull up my sock and liner. People sometimes stare or slow down and honk as they drive by. Instead of feeling embarrassed, though, pride swells up inside me when I consider all the amazing adventures I've had in the sport and the miles I'm about to cover.

I have a photo of the first time I wore a bikini on the beach as an amputee. It was 2016, fifteen years after my surgery and early on in my running journey. I was sitting on my towel, covered up as usual. But Eliza begged me to come swim with her, so I gathered all my courage, left my long garments behind, and waded into the water. Some people pointed and stared, but one kind woman—a stranger—walked up and told me, "You are beautiful." I cried, then smiled as I realized I believed her.

Running has changed my body physically, of course—I'm stronger and fitter than I've ever been. But even more than that, it's taught me that the way you look has little to do with who you are or how much you're worth. You are not defined, even as a runner, by your physique, which clothes you wear, or the pace or distance you travel. Rather, it's the mere act of trying—your drive to be the best version of yourself—that brings you the small wins that then accumulate into sweeping transformations.

6

RISE ABOVE THE HATERS

Marathon 35 of 104

If there's one day of the 104 I'd rather forget, it's day 35.

Weekends were always a bit off the routine, and this Sunday, it was even more different than usual. Edwin and I began the day by running the Lost Dutchman Half Marathon, a race in a park a little less than an hour away from home.

I hadn't done any other official races while I was going for my record, choosing instead to mostly stick around home and to my own schedule, a plan that allowed me more time to recover between efforts. However, this race was so close that it seemed fine to squeeze it in. I truly appreciated the change of scenery, the company, and the music along the course, not to mention the cool medal in the shape of a saguaro cactus.

Since moving to Arizona in 2021, I'd come to love running beside these spiky giants; though I see them nearly every day, I can't help but stop to take photos of them regularly. They can grow up to fifty feet tall and live for as long as two hundred years, and they have adapted to the Sonoran Desert's harsh climate by soaking up as much water as they can each time it rains. In my mind, they're true models of endurance, adaptation, and resilience.

Edwin finished the race in 1:32:40, winning his age group. I took my time, coming in about an hour behind him. I still had energy to spare, but because we had to get back to the kiddos, I couldn't just keep going.

So we drove home and, not too long after, I headed out for another 13.1 miles around the neighborhood. After that, I was done for the day…or so I thought. I posted about my efforts—with a race photo and a mention of how I'd divided the day's 26.2 distance—on Instagram.

As is often the case, the vast majority of comments were supportive. Some people mentioned that doing two half marathons was probably even harder than running a full. I was inclined to agree; getting started again after coming to a full stop was *tough*.

But then there were a few comments that shook me. "Does two half marathons count?" "Are you *sure* you checked the rules?" "You have to do the whole 26.2 at once."

Sitting on the couch mid-scroll, I began to panic. Had I put my attempt in jeopardy? My heart pounded as I went to my computer. When you apply to pursue a Guinness World Record, you set up an online account. After you log in, on your application page you'll find a link to the guidelines governing your specific record. I headed there, opened the guidelines, read them, and then read them again. As far as I could tell, they only specified that I had to complete a marathon-distance course in a day, not that all the miles had to be consecutive. I called Edwin over. I figured, with his detail-oriented approach to all things, he'd be able to help me get to the bottom of the matter.

"I think you're right," he said. "But I can also see the other side of the argument. It isn't clear at all."

Now I was worried. The last thing I wanted was to have to stop and start over—or, worse, to keep going but then get disqualified on a technicality. I knew from social media that others were going for this record too, and that I was likely to lose out if I was interrupted. Guinness would clarify the rules if I asked, but they'd take days, if not weeks, to respond. It was already late afternoon; I didn't have time to wait.

So, I put my blade back on and started running. Again.

I have no idea how I managed another 26.2 miles in 24 hours. Much of it is a blur. At that point, I was fueled by fear and rage, chasing the beam of my headlamp on the sidewalk in front of me.

I finished at 11:55 p.m., exhausted, after completing a total of 52.4 miles for the day. I sank into bed without even bothering to shower. My leg and stump both cramped, making it difficult to sleep. I wasn't sure what tomorrow would bring. Would I even be able to run? No matter what, I'd given it my best effort, silencing my critics and my own doubts.

~

I try to keep things positive for the most part, but this was far from my first experience of people questioning me in person or online. Each time it happens, it brings to mind a series of memories that stick with me, starting with some from not long after I started running in 2016.

That fall, I had just finished my first 5K on a running blade, pushing the limits of my temporary test socket. I was thrilled with how it went; now that I had the right equipment, I'd made tremendous progress. I walked up to the race director, who was holding what looked like a printout of finishing times. "Mind if I take a peek?" I asked.

She looked me up and down and, without even glancing at the paper in her hands, and said, "You won't be on this list because this list is for winners."

My jaw dropped. I backed away. Clearly, she didn't think someone running with a blade was capable of performing well. Later on, I looked up my results online. I had won my age group.

And then there's a whole other line of interrogation that's come up several times since 2016. I was in the start corral before a 5K when two other runners, a mother and daughter—the girl probably about eight years old—approached me to ask about my prosthetic. Since many people aren't familiar with the technology, I'm always happy to answer well-intentioned questions. If nothing else, I figured, chatting would take my mind off my pre-race nerves.

At first, they were curious about what it was made of and how it fit. A few minutes in, though, the conversation took a turn. "Are you sure you're actually allowed to compete in these races?" the woman asked. "Because surely your blade gives you an advantage."

"Wait—whaaaa?" I thought. I was simultaneously shocked and embarrassed. The very thought was bizarre. If only she knew how hard I'd worked, the blisters and blood, the money I'd spent. I didn't regain my composure enough to answer before the starting gun.

As all the runners around us took off, I lost the mom and her daughter in the crowd. I tried to put the incident out of my mind and focus on running, but as I neared the finish line, I could see the mom just ahead of me. Rather than push to catch her, I held back. We were in the same age group; if I passed her, I feared I'd confirm her accusations of my cheating.

This same issue came up again the next year, when I was preparing for my third half marathon, which would be held on the American Tobacco Trail in North Carolina. I felt extremely fortunate to be training there, on the race course. The wide, paved path follows an old railroad track, and it's popular among locals.

One day, an older couple on bikes came from the opposite direction and slowed down, motioning to me. I had headphones on and couldn't hear them at first. I wondered if they needed help, if something had gone wrong. I paused my music and asked, "Are you okay?"

It was the man who answered. "I read that you are not allowed to compete in races, because you cheat by running on a prosthetic leg," he said.

I actually looked around for a video crew at that point, wondering if I was on some hidden-camera joke show. But no, this couple had decided to stop their bike ride solely to accuse me of misconduct in some hypothetical competition. I wasn't sure what they wanted me to do—confess to some crime? Return my (nonexistent) Olympic medals? Stop running and hop into a wheelchair instead? I smiled weakly, turned the volume back up, and ran away.

Years later, in 2023, I was struggling a bit through the 100K at the Javelina Jundred. It was two days before Halloween, and I was dressed appropriately: in an orange shirt and an orange tutu with a jack-o'-lantern face on it. But while my attire might have been lighthearted, my mood was dark. This was one of those days when it seemed like absolutely *nothing* was going my way. The heat sapped my energy and made me sweat more than usual. My liner sock had folded over, cutting into my skin, and my stump was bleeding. As the race wore on, my quads and hamstrings kept cramping up, so I stopped nearly every mile to release my blade and rub my stump, easing the pain. One of those times, I put it back on incorrectly and the suction held my leg in the wrong place, creating a huge blister.

At one point, I sat on a rock and cried with frustration. I hated struggling so much with my stupid prosthetic—and yes, I called it stupid in my head. I'll admit, this was not my finest moment for positive self-talk! Then, as I tried to get up, I nearly fell—because I forgot I'd taken my leg off.

I got up, put my leg back on, and gathered my composure. As I slogged along near the back of the pack, another runner ambled up beside me. "You have a huge advantage with that prosthetic," he said, without a touch of irony. Now, I'm not encouraging aggressive behavior, but I'll admit to a brief moment in which I wondered if I'd be disqualified for punching a fellow competitor.

Day 35 was a real doozy, but it wasn't the only time online comments got to me. As more people started paying attention to my multi-marathon effort, more trolls emerged from the depths of the internet. I don't want to sound ungrateful, because so many of my followers were kind and supportive—but that only made the ones that weren't stand out even more.

Here are some of my not-so-favorite comments:

"It isn't fair because she doesn't get foot pain like we do. The 104 consecutive marathons was easier for her."

"You should be disqualified because you have an advantage."

"I'm tired of seeing posts by people with disabilities. It makes me uncomfortable."

And then, the one that nearly made me throw my phone across the room: "You make running look so easy, I think I'm going to have my leg amputated."

Sometimes, it seems I can't win. When you lose a limb as an adult, you see clearly how people's perceptions of you change. You're disabled, you're labeled. People want to put you in a box. In some cases, that means treating you as an object of pity or ignoring you altogether. My mind flashes back to so many conversations when I've been overlooked or left out, both in the running community and outside of it.

Some people, seeing only my disability and not my ability, feel inspired to "help." I can't tell you how many times I've had seemingly well-intentioned people offer to assist me in stepping off a curb or climbing up stairs. I mean, sure, it's nice to hold a door open for someone or ask what they need if they're struggling, but when I'm just going about my day, someone trying to help me with basic tasks feels like they assume I am utterly incompetent. I typically offer a polite "no thank you" and go about my business, even if I'm tempted to show them my ultramarathon medals.

Running was part of my way of pushing back on this narrative. But then just as I began finding my footing, I was accused of cheating.

The first time this happened, with the mother and daughter, I was so gobsmacked I couldn't begin to process what was happening. I'd fought so hard to get to the starting line. The idea that some people would honestly think I had a leg up—pun completely intended—did not compute.

Then, I got mad. *Really* mad.

However, once I moved through my initial shock and anger, I started to get curious about what was behind these accusations. If I could understand where people were coming from with this misconception of me having an advantage, maybe I could help bridge the gap.

Part of the issue, I think, is rooted in the same discrimination and false ideas about people with disabilities that lead some strangers to try to help me with basic tasks. If you think I'm helpless, I can see why you'd be shocked—or even suspect there's some sort of shadiness at play—when I run up and down mountains.

Another layer, I've realized, is a lack of education. Some people truly do not know better, or they know just enough about running to have some misconceptions. They might have heard something about carbon fiber supershoes, or double amputees being barred from competition, and get things twisted in a way that just isn't right.

And then there's pure jealousy. No matter what your endeavor, if you have some degree of success, there will always be people who question you or try to tear you down. That's even more true on social media, where anyone can hide behind a keyboard and a pseudonym (although some people have allowed that boldness to filter out into the real world too). There are also people who, when they see someone like me who's overcome obstacles, feel guilt and shame about their own perceived failures. Instead of dealing with their emotions or working on their own lives, they lash out at me. It would be great if more people went to therapy, or started running themselves, or did whatever else it was they needed to do to avoid being huge jerks to those of us who are out here trying our best. In the meantime, we're all damaged by their outbursts.

As for how I deal with the negativity, all I can say is that I'm human. I can't control the fact that I have a negative emotional reaction to these types of comments, criticisms, and baseless allegations. You might find me screaming in my living room as I read them, or shutting down if they're delivered in person.

With time and effort, though, as I've come to understand more about where certain people are coming from, I've learned that while it's hard to control how I feel about these comments, I can choose how I respond. My first line of defense is taking care of myself. That might mean stepping away from the person speaking to me, closing Instagram, or phoning a friend.

During the marathon streak, it was sometimes harder to do this, because I wanted to stay engaged on social media; so many people were following my journey, including others with disabilities and challenges, and I believed I owed it to them not only to run my best but also to stand up to bullies who tried to drag me down.

Whenever someone posted a comment that riled me up, I'd often speak with my friend Rachel Zelibor back in North Carolina. We'd run side by side for miles when I lived there, and even when I moved away, we stayed close. She's always cool and collected, whereas I'm a bit more emotional. Whenever I got angry, she helped me put things in perspective, reassuring me both that my emotions were valid and also that I didn't have to let them carry me down into a negative spiral. Edwin, too, often provides a pragmatic counterpoint. He's seen all my struggles and reminds me that other people don't have the full set of facts.

Rachel and Edwin both helped me craft my post about my second marathon on day 35. I wanted to share what had happened without dipping into blame or shame. "After my post I had a few people say that marathon 35 didn't count, because I split it up and that's against the 'rules.' The rules only say you need to complete a marathon distance in a day," I wrote. "To be safe I decided to run it again and this time I didn't split it, so yes I ran 2 marathons in 24 hours." On Rachel and Edwin's advice, I disabled the comments on the post. I needed the final word this time.

Another part of my strategy is to educate. I fully recognize that sometimes, in a bid to keep things upbeat, my social media presence makes it look like running comes easily to me. So I aim to balance this out with posts that also show the challenges—the times when sweat makes my leg slide off mid-workout, when the bones of my stump shift in a way that causes pain and swelling, when my skin breaks down and blisters, and when I'm dealing with the exorbitant costs of not only each running blade (goodbye, $10,000 to $20,000) but also the new socket I need to order every year because all the miles I put in have worn the old one out.

I also aim to correct underlying myths and misunderstandings. For instance, those in the running community often conflate the carbon fiber that running blades are made of with the carbon fiber plates inside next-generation racing shoes, commonly referred to as supershoes. Studies show these racing shoes can improve what's called running economy—a measure of how much oxygen it takes you to run each mile—by, in some cases, 4 percent to 7 percent. That means people wearing them can either run faster at the same effort level or hold a given pace for longer.

These shoes—which, by the way, are legal in competition, with some guidelines—are part of a technological and training revolution that has caused world records to fall in both track and road racing. Some people reason (incorrectly) that if a plated shoe can do that, a whole carbon fiber blade must offer even more of a boost.

There are several reasons why this argument holds no water. Interestingly, the more research that scientists conduct on supershoes, the more they realize it's not the carbon fiber plates that actually improve race times. Rather, the secret sauce is that these plates allow shoe manufacturers to pile shoes higher with more foam, in formulations that are lighter and bouncier. Shoe companies give these foams names like "Boost" and "Nitro" because they offer what's called superior energy return: They take some of the force of your foot striking against the ground and give it back to you to power your next stride forward. That's why World Athletics, the governing body of track and field, has rules that limit what's called the stack height of these shoes, since the more foam you stack up, the greater the energy return.

If you look at a running blade, you'll see no such cushioning. Comparing supershoes to blades is like comparing apples to oranges, or more like apples to spinach or ceiling fans or zebras. The two things aren't at all related. Don't feel bad if you found this confusing before; you're far from alone. I've even had conversations with knowledgeable shoe-company execs who misunderstood these facts.

Another misleading line of thinking has to do with double amputees like Blake Leeper, who was banned from competing in the Tokyo Olympics in 2021 due to questions about whether his two blades gave him a competitive edge over athletes with two legs. The research in this area has been fascinating but far from conclusive. A study that suggested Oscar Pistorius, another double amputee, could run the same speed with less energy prevented him from competing in the 2008 Games, but a later report found his abilities were similar to those of runners who don't use prosthetic legs, even if his mechanics were a bit different. As a result, he was allowed to line up at the London Games in 2012.

After that, however, World Athletics decided that each individual athlete would have the burden of proving their prosthetics didn't give them a boost. Leeper enlisted the help of the same researcher who'd studied Pistorius, University of Colorado Boulder's Alena Grabowski. Her research showed that he and other bilateral amputees had no advantage and that they had never run faster than top non-amputee runners in any lab tests of sprinting ability. In fact, sprinters with two blades showed several deficits, including that they were 40 percent slower out of the starting blocks and 1 to 3 percent slower around curves than runners with two flesh-and-blood legs.

Despite those results, Leeper still wasn't allowed to run in Tokyo; officials said his blades made him too tall. This is an ongoing area of controversy, with athletes, scientists, and officials alike debating the fairness of calculations that dictate what's called maximum allowable standing height for competition.

I find this science fascinating, and I'm always glad to discuss it with people who are engaging in good faith. However, I ask them to keep in mind that I'm a unilateral amputee—a single blade is a whole different ball game.

Yes, running blades act as springs, but so do the human foot and calf. All my blade does is replicate the basic mechanics required to run, allowing me to take part in the activity like anyone else. And if you take a moment to think about the mechanics involved, you can see why it couldn't possibly be advantageous to have one leg and one blade.

Running is essentially a series of single-legged hops. As I stride, I push off from the blade on my left side, land on my right foot, then push off on my right foot before landing on my blade. Even if my blade was somehow supercharged—and believe me, it's not—my other leg would somehow have to become even faster to keep up with it in order to give me an overall increase in speed. Plus, active prosthetics are typically designed with the needs of male athletes in mind. I've actually been a part of a study in Colorado done by researchers who pointed out that they don't always work as well as they could for women. We may need further adjustments—for instance, blades that aren't quite as stiff—to run their best. In other words, rather than having a leg up (ha), wearing a blade as a woman is just another obstacle in my way.

Once I got through the initial process of learning to trust my blade, I realized there was a lot more I had to do to run healthy for the long term. The first few years I ran, I didn't realize that I was putting far more pressure and weight on my full leg than on my stump and my blade. Eventually, I could even see that my right thigh was much bigger and more muscular than my left. With help and guidance from physical therapists, I've worked hard on strength training, including movements like single-leg deadlifts, to balance my gait. I also have to continuously strengthen and stretch my hip flexors, which take a bit more of a beating because of the pounding of the blade.

No matter how hard I work in the gym, my blade will never have the flexibility and agility of my missing foot and ankle. I still can't feel it when my foot strikes the ground or hits a root or rock—at least not until my blade catches and twists, a sensation that's not unlike a twisting or spraining an ankle. And then there's the chafing and blisters and equipment failure I encounter along the way.

Purely from a physiological standpoint, I use about 20 percent more energy to run than someone without a prosthetic. And that doesn't even account for the mental bandwidth I have to use to advocate for myself in places where runners with disabilities haven't previously been welcomed, or to argue with people who have false ideas about what it means to run with a blade.

~

When I share all these things, I'm not looking for sympathy or any sort of handout or consolation prize. I've chosen to push my limits, and I've proven, time and again, that I have what it takes to exceed them. What I want is for people to understand that there's a real person behind my social media accounts and race results, one who's worked damn hard for all she's accomplished. Yes, the blade has allowed me to run, and I'll be forever grateful. But in no way has it vaulted me ahead of the competition.

Every runner faces unique burdens and challenges when they set out to achieve their goals. The barriers we must hurdle over as para-athletes are significant in every way—physically, logistically, emotionally, and financially. Whether it's me or another amputee you see in a starting corral or at the finish line, I hope you'll think twice about your underlying assumptions and feel a greater degree of respect for and understanding of our efforts.

I often find this type of education goes down more easily with a bit of humor. Sometimes, merely repeating the posts or comments I get makes them funnier automatically. I mean, come on—who is truly going to have their leg amputated to get better at running? It's so absurd, it's humorous, and bringing such nonsense out into the open takes away much of its power.

I'll also make jokes about the few "advantages" I do have. For example, many ultrarunners lose toenails because of the hours of microtrauma their nails undergo as they hit the upper of their shoes. So yes, it's true, I admit it: I'm lucky to have only five toenails to sacrifice. I might also point out that when it's rainy and muddy, only one foot gets wet. You know, the important things!

As for the pure trolls—those who find joy in tearing others down, or who deal with their shortcomings by dragging others to their level—I find the best response is to just keep doing what I'm doing. You'll never make everyone happy, I've learned, so it's best to stop trying. Instead, focus on the one person whose happiness you have the most influence over: you.

If those types of people have you doubting yourself, I hope my example provides both knowledge and realistic hope. Doing big, scary things isn't always easy, but that shouldn't stop you from trying. You might have to get creative and resourceful, but that's something you do all the time. The payoff of going for your goals is worth it, and I'm here to help you along the way.

It's also tempting, when you get blowback, to hide what you're doing or try to fade into the woodwork. Believe me, I've been there; there are plenty of days when I feel like deleting my social media altogether or going back to my days of long pants and hiding in the shadows. But there are many reasons to overcome these urges. One, for me, is the hot Arizona sun; wearing shorts is far more comfortable and practical! I also know I've helped many more people by showing and talking about my prosthetic than I ever did when I hid it. Because of health problems like diabetes and a preponderance of motorcycle accidents, there are a lot of amputees here in the Phoenix area, and when people can see me and ask questions about my prosthetics and my training, I know it gives them what they need to be more active too.

In any case, you should never let other people's ideas of what you can or should do define you. Your light in the world shines brightest when you're doing what makes you feel the most alive. Let the haters' harsh words fuel you, thinking of how mad they'll be when you set a new goal or power through to another finish line.

Sometimes, when I'm feeling tired or unmotivated, I think of that race director way back from my first 5K. When I remember how she told me I wasn't a winner without even bothering to check, I find the drive to go a little farther and push a little harder. If I ever meet her again, I'll thank her for what she's done for me. Then, of course, I'll sprint away to the next challenge.

Case in point, on day 36 of the marathon challenge, the day after the double, my stump was a little swollen and my blade didn't fit perfectly as a result. Although I was tired, I made it through the next set of miles, in large part because I'd received so much support from my family, friends, and fans. If you, like me, doubt yourself, know this: The kindness you'll inspire just by being yourself can boost you above everyone who might try to drag you down.

7

DON'T OVERLOOK THE BASICS

Marathon 39 of 104

"Onions," I thought. "That's what would taste really good to me right now."

I was just about to finish marathon 39. And I have to say, the thought surprised me. Who knocks out 26.2 miles and craves not a burger and fries or a burrito but a pungent bulb-shaped vegetable? I'd noticed more of these unusual pangs lately—some days I craved yogurt, others buffalo wings. "There has to be something to this," I said to myself.

With some Googling, I started to peel back the layers. Food cravings could be a sign from my body that I was lacking certain important nutrients, I learned. Some sources suggested a taste for onions meant I needed more vitamin C, and pining for yogurt might mean I was low in calcium or protein. The wings were a bit more of a stumper, until I saw that many people crave spicy foods when they're overheating. (Some of the ingredients first make you sweat, then cool you down, apparently.)

Well, I couldn't do much about that one, except turn to the treadmill when the Arizona heat was at its most brutal. The rest, however, was more than food for thought; it gave me some helpful guidance to revamp my fueling strategy.

Running 100-plus marathons in a row is a significant challenge, but alongside that is an equally daunting effort: eating to power those thousands of miles.

At first, I took on this part of the quest enthusiastically but with little direction. I assumed that because I was running so much, I could eat whatever I wanted and be fine—bags of chips for snacks, ice cream for a meal, entire pizzas. During my runs, I took fluids and gels, aiming for 150 calories per hour, a calculation I'd used in the past during marathons and ultramarathons.

Somewhere around the one-month mark, I realized this strategy wasn't working for me. Not only did I get cravings but, for a few mornings in a row, I had zero energy when I woke up. "Jacky," you might be thinking, "you were running a marathon a day. Of course you were tired!" I mean, yes, some level of fatigue was bound to occur. But this exhaustion felt different, like it was coming from deep inside my cells.

Athletes always talk about listening to their bodies, but sometimes it's hard to know exactly what that means. In this case, mine was delivering loud and clear messages about what it needed and wasn't getting. I just needed to learn to speak its language.

With Edwin's help, I made a plan to eat more strategically. Remember how I told you that ultrarunners often eat solid foods during super-long distances? I brought that approach to my everyday marathons, upping my goal to around 200 calories per hour, and getting more of those calories through foods like potatoes and peanut butter sandwiches. Not only did they provide more filling fiber and protein, they were also rich in minerals such as potassium and magnesium, which support muscle repair and function.

Off the run, I kept in mind that each meal had to both help me recover from my previous effort and prepare me for my next one. I ate even more than before, and I also made each meal higher quality. I focused on three main areas: protein to rebuild my tired muscles; high-quality carbs to replenish the glycogen—the fuel source stored within muscles—that I'd expended the day before; and antioxidants, plentiful in fruits and veggies, to fight cell damage and calm the inflammation that occurs with intense exercise.

Instead of reaching for whatever I could find in the snack cabinet when I got home, I ate yogurt and berries, which together are rich in protein and antioxidants like vitamin C, anthocyanins, and flavanols. If I wasn't hungry—which can happen when you're running in the heat—I blended everything up in a shake, adding a handful of spinach for an extra boost of iron, calcium, and fiber. Dinners were something like rice and black beans with avocado, corn, salsa, and chicken.

Mind you, I didn't focus on banishing foods like pizza and ice cream; restriction isn't the way out of underfueling, especially if you have a history of eating disorders or disordered eating. (Often, when journalists would interview me about my marathon challenge, they'd ask if I had lost weight. I was always puzzled by this; obviously, that was far from the point, and my whole goal was to eat enough that I wasn't in a calorie deficit and could maintain the strength and muscle mass to continue!) Instead, I prioritized adding the things I needed, keeping the treats I adored as the tip of the pyramid on top of a solid base of nutrient-dense options.

Within a few days, the changes began to pay off. Each day's effort left me less depleted, I slept better at night, and I woke up each morning with a bit more pep. My muscles, while still tired, felt less sore and stiff. And in a change that somewhat surprised me, but shouldn't have, my mood and motivation improved too.

~

I've said it before and I'll say it again: Your mind is critical to tackling long distances. If I had to break it down, I'd say running is about 80 percent mental and 20 percent physical. So many of the challenges you'll face during long hours on the roads and trails are psychological—from crippling self-doubt and the fear of failure to low motivation and even boredom.

However, just as the mental influences the physical, the reverse is also true. Your brain is a part of your body, after all. The better you attend to your body's needs as a matter of habit, the more mental energy you have to coach yourself through the tough spots and keep yourself going. And sometimes a problem that presents as an emotional crisis springs out of a relatively simple physical need for food, sleep, or just a few deep breaths.

I can't tell you how many times I've thought, "I can't go on," eaten a peanut butter sandwich, and then found my will to continue. When fear creeps in, as it did before the Stairway to Heaven section of the VK, deep breathing can reset the nervous system and deliver essential oxygen to your brain and your muscles. And then, there's the life-changing power of the nap.

~

December 2022

I came to Across the Years—a running festival that spans six days between December and January—with a clear goal. It was just a couple of months after I finished my record-breaking marathon streak. For all I'd accomplished in my running career up to that point, there was one achievement that thus far had eluded me: conquering 200 miles. The distance had been on my mind since early in my ultrarunning career, but every time I'd gotten close to completing it, I hit a setback—an equipment malfunction, poor weather, an injury, or just plain bad luck.

My most recent thwarted attempt was the Moab 240 race in October of 2022. In the aftermath of the marathon record, life had gotten a bit hectic. Between recovery, press interviews, and picking up some family responsibilities I'd let slide, I wasn't doing all the training I'd planned. And then, I had a freak accident—a fall in the shower. That hadn't happened to me in years; I'd slipped, and when I instinctively stuck my left leg out to steady myself, my foot and ankle weren't there. I slammed down on my stump, hard.

When I went to the emergency room, the doctors weren't quite sure what to make of me. My stump was so swollen that I couldn't put my pin-and-socket walking foot on, so I had to wear my running blade, which has a slightly wider socket and a suction system. They worried I'd broken a bone, since the pain was so intense and I don't have a lot of muscle, fat, or other tissue cushioning my tibia.

Fortunately, X-rays showed no break; it was just badly bruised. So, too, was my ego. At this point, I had sponsors funding my running endeavors, and I had to tell them that I couldn't run either the Leadville 100, which I'd planned to do in August, or Moab in October. And, I had to tell them why. "Sure, I can run up and down mountains, but put me in a shower and I'm done for," I thought.

Fortunately, all my sponsors were incredibly kind about it. After I threw myself a bit of a pity party, I took a step back and reconsidered my situation. In reality, the accident was probably my body's sign that I needed a break, that I was putting a bit too much pressure on myself. I listened, and let myself heal.

~

By September, I was running pain-free again. The Moab race was the following month, but I wouldn't have had time to safely build back up for it, especially given how remote and challenging the course was. Runners there loop through mountains, canyons, and parkland, with more than 30,000 feet of climbing along the way. If I were to fall or get lost, rescue crews would have to come after me. Going to a race like that undertrained would put others in danger too. I had to let that dream go, at least for now.

But Across the Years, which wasn't until December, offered the perfect opportunity for a 200-mile redemption. Like the Fat Ox, it involves a lot of laps of a short distance—in this case, a loop just under a mile long at Camelback Ranch–Glendale. Runners can choose the length of their race, from six hours to six days. Because we ultrarunners are always aiming to challenge ourselves in new ways, there's also a "last person standing," or "backyard," category. In that one, runners start a lap every 20 minutes, aiming to maintain at least a 15-minute-mile pace. The person who can keep that up for the longest without stopping is declared the victor. That year, the man who won ran more than 140 miles that way!

I chose the full six-day, 144-hour race. Runner math told me that since 200 miles was what I wanted, I needed to average about 34 miles per day. Given that I'd just run 26.2 miles for more than 100 days, that sounded incredibly doable. In between, I could stop and rest on a cot in a tent on the ranch grounds.

The course was about an hour away from home, so while I wasn't going to ask Edwin to stay out there with me the entire six days, he could easily go back and forth to be there as much as he could—running some laps with me, waiting by the tent to help me with gear or food, and even at one point getting me an In-N-Out Burger that I wolfed down. It felt like the perfect setup to finally secure that 200-mile buckle.

What I didn't account for was the weather. The first two days, it poured. "Just my luck," I thought. Fortunately, I'd at least checked the forecast and bought a canopy for the outside of my tent, so I could set my food and gear down without it getting soaked. The race has proper aid stations, just like at Fat Ox, and they serve snacks throughout the day as well as full meals: French toast and pancakes for breakfast, sandwiches or hot dogs for lunch, and lasagna, pizza, or burritos for dinner. However, I still wanted to make sure I had food to quell my own cravings too. Among my stash were M&M's, gummy worms, and sweet cookies called Stroopwafels.

Now, you might be asking: "Didn't you just say, Jacky, that you needed more nutritious foods to survive multiple marathons?" While my hoard of junk food might seem like a contradiction to that philosophy, the situations were quite different. When you're running six days straight, your body doesn't really have time to rebuild and recover; everything you take in goes directly to fuel your running. So, the most important thing in most ultraraces is getting the calories and energy to continue. At first, I approached the 100-marathon challenge that way too. However, when I was continuing that degree of activity for months and with nearly a full day of rest in between each effort, I learned I had to give my body better building blocks to recover. This race, though, was just about getting through in the moment.

With my fueling strategy set, and despite the downpour, I powered through the first day. I hit my goal of 34 miles. While I probably should have stopped then, my competitive side kicked in, and I kept going. Before I knew it, I had hit 51 miles. It was time to take a break for the night.

I knew my blade was slipping a bit in the mud, but I didn't quite realize until I stopped and started up again how much this was affecting my gait. Often, when I'm doing long distances—especially in tough conditions—the fibula of my amputated leg shifts a bit and the back of my knee swells up. This time, I somehow bruised my knee as well. The pain in my stump meant I was favoring my good leg more than usual, putting more strain and pressure on my muscles, joints, and ligaments. My right shin and ankle swelled up in protest. Both my legs ached.

As tired as I was when I lay down to rest, sleep didn't come easily. Desert nights are cold, and the rain made everything damp. On my cot in the tent, the chill seeped into my bones through my sleeping bag. Edwin was kind enough to bring me a heavy duvet from home, which helped a little with my body temperature, but I still couldn't drift off. Much of the time I was stopped, I was merely resting, not actually sleeping. At least my mind got a brief break from the effort of pushing forward.

And that, it turned out, was the most important thing. As the days wore on, I learned to tell when I needed to stop, which was when I was at my most grumpy and moody, snapping at Edwin or doubting what I was even doing there or whether I could continue. Each time I began to feel that darkness bubble up, I headed to the tent for a two-hour respite. Afterward, I found myself able to move forward.

As the days wore on, the challenges didn't quit. The rain seeped under the tread attached to my blade, and the strip of material simply fell right off all at once, without even the warning of loosening gradually, as it usually does. Bare carbon on gravel isn't a good situation, so I did what I could, using my shoelace to tie the tread back on until I could get back to my tent and my trusty duct tape.

There were moments during this race when I could barely keep my eyes open, but I kept plodding. My knee was so stiff and swollen that eventually I couldn't bend it at all. I shuffled much of the way, switching between my walking foot and running blade. I still struggled to sleep. (Ironically, one of the few times I did doze off, I missed the New Year's celebration, when race organizers handed out nonalcoholic champagne to welcome in 2023.) The miles somehow kept ticking off, and by the final day, I had only 27 to go.

After all I'd been through, that last push might just have been the most challenging. Edwin had brought the kids that day, so they could see me finish. Around mile 195, as close as I was, I somehow became convinced I could go no farther. I sat down by my tent, where they were waiting for me, and cried. "I don't want to go anymore," I told Edwin.

"You've come so far, Jacky," he said. "It's just a few more miles."

I wasn't having it. "If you want to finish this, *you* go finish it!" I yelled back. "I'm done. I'm not getting to 200. It's all over."

Now, Edwin was also an expert in the inner workings of Jacky—he'd been paying attention the previous few days (not to mention the entire two decades we'd been together)—and he knew grumpy, angry Jacky wasn't the one most in touch with what I truly wanted.

"Jacky, you need a nap," he told me firmly. "Go take one." I headed to the tent, angry and exhausted.

That thirty minutes might have been the deepest sleep I had the whole week. Even Edwin and Eliza couldn't wake me at first. Gradually, I roused myself and regrouped my thoughts. Those few winks cleared my thinking and gave me a whole new perspective.

"Jacky, look at what you've overcome—in your life, and just in these last six days," I told myself. "That dream you have, it's right in front of you. Let's go get it."

The final laps weren't pretty—it was late, nearly 10:00 p.m., and I was hurting—but I just kept going. The kids did the last two loops with me, though they knew to swerve away right before I finished,

so Edwin could get video of me crossing the timing mat one last time. The feeling when I finally did, and when a volunteer handed me a giant silver 200-mile buckle, can only be described as ecstasy. Obviously, things hadn't gone quite the way I'd planned, but there were so many times when I could have stepped off the course—and I didn't. Thanks in part to the power of the nap, I'd persevered, and I was proud and grateful.

~

Ultrarunning often demands that we draw on our deepest reserves of creativity and mental strength. However, before we can even get to those higher levels of problem-solving and persevering, it sure helps to make sure you've eaten, slept, and tended to your other basic needs. Sometimes I've learned this the hard way, when overlooking a basic biological or logistical reality has made it impossible for me to continue.

Take my second attempt at the Umstead 100-miler, in 2023. I'd been sick a couple of weeks before and had unintentionally lost weight all over my body, including my stump. As a result, the suction that holds on my prosthetic was loose, causing painful rubbing and chafing. An extra sock would have helped, but I didn't carry one on me. I had a crew with more supplies, including another sock, but I couldn't meet up with them until after the first of eight 12.5-mile loops.

By the time I got to the end of that lap and met up with my team—including my dear friend Jeannette, who's always on top of every detail, as well as my buddies Sam, Lori, and Gray—the damage was done. At that point, I switched to my walking leg and tried my best to continue. But even with all the support and encouragement, I fell behind on time, missed the cutoff, and had to stop at mile 75. I was proud to have pushed as long as I did, but no amount of mental resilience could overcome the physical existence of my raw, blistered skin.

Some of your basic needs will differ from mine. Others are universal: air, food, water, sleep, clothing, and potty breaks. When you're feeling overwhelmed, it's helpful to treat yourself like a parent would a child in the middle of a tantrum. In a calm, soothing tone, ask yourself: Do I need a snack? Should I lie down? Would a few deep breaths help me regain control and continue moving forward?

In moments of deep fear and despair, covering the basics can bring clarity and restore our higher-level, analytical minds. That way, we can solve bigger problems. Honestly, sometimes taking care of those needs is the solution itself. After a well-balanced meal or a thirty-minute nap, what once seemed unfathomable is suddenly possible again.

8

BE YOUR OWN ADVOCATE

Marathon 50 of 104

There are two kinds of runners in the world. You can tell them apart by watching what happens when they reach the end of a run and see a distance of 5.98 or 9.97 on their GPS watch. Some will be chill enough to stop without a thought. Others will run back and forth around a parking lot or past their own driveway to hit an even 6 or 10 miles. I'm in the second category, at least when I'm not doing a challenge that involves stopping at a specific number, like 26.2.

There's just some mystical allure to big, round numbers. That's what compelled me to go for 100 marathons in the first place, as daunting as it sounded. On March 7, 2022, I hit a huge milestone: the halfway point, 50 marathons.

You know how I feel about celebrating smaller wins along the way. For this one, I figured I'd ask my social media followers to help me mark the occasion. A couple of days beforehand, I posted on Instagram requesting that they join me. They didn't have to run a marathon, but I asked that they do anything active with "50" in it. Fifty squats, 50 push-ups, 50 minutes of running or walking—whatever would make them feel good.

I loved scrolling the #50withJacky hashtag afterward. Besides 50-minute runs, people got creative. One athlete completed 50 reps each of ten different strength exercises, adding another 50 pounds of weight to her squats and deadlifts. A mom recruited her two sons to do 50 jumping jacks, 50 push-ups, and 50 sit-ups. A runner set a goal of covering 50,000 steps in a day and crushed it. One woman rode 50 miles on her indoor spin bike—it took her two and a half hours—and a pair of coaches in North Carolina did 50 jumps with a two-pound jump rope.

Seeing their support and encouragement filled me up. And I needed it because, to be honest, day 50 was about as close as I'd come so far to quitting. That nice, round number hung there in front of me, taunting me. "People would get it if you stopped now," an inner voice piped up inside me. "You can be proud of yourself for 50 marathons in a row."

And while it's true I had already done a lot, I knew, if I was being honest, that this voice didn't represent my deeper wishes. I envisioned what it would be like to post the next day that my journey had concluded early. I thought about how far I'd already come. Then, I pulled up the GoFundMe I'd set up for Amputee Blade

Runners. So far, people had donated enough to cover almost two blades at $10,000 each.

Amputees who want to get into running or other sports have enough obstacles in their way already. I'm always telling them—and everyone—they can do more than they think, more than they believe. I've encouraged them to step outside their comfort zones so many times, to fight for what they want, to follow their dreams. If continuing would harm me—if I was injured or sick—that was one thing. Otherwise, I felt like I owed it to them to "keep showing up," as Olympic marathoner and 2018 Boston Marathon champion Des Linden always says.

And, what's more, I owed it to myself. I knew how much confidence and strength I always gained from continuing when my mind wanted me to quit. I needed to show up for myself too.

On day 51, I got out of bed, got the kids off to school, and got myself out the door, again.

~

June 2020

I stood in my North Carolina kitchen, getting ready to make some lunch. I wore my usual walking foot, the one I'd had since we moved from the United Kingdom. As I took a step forward toward the refrigerator, my foot—and my sense of security—shattered beneath me.

I'd spent two decades training my brain to trust my prosthetic, and now, it had failed me. Fear gripped me as I began to tumble.

Would I have to start building that trust all over again? Fortunately, I was close enough to the kitchen table to grab the edge and prevent myself from falling flat on my face.

Edwin, who was working from home when heard a thump and a few choice curse words, rushed over to me. "Jacky! Are you okay? What happened?" he asked as he helped me to a chair.

"I have no idea, but I'm sitting here and my foot is over there," I answered. He picked it up and saw that the mechanism that controls the height and attaches the pylon, or the metal shaft, to the foot had completely snapped off. And inside the foot shell, the other pieces were shattered.

I was shocked—but perhaps I shouldn't have been. My prosthetic was one of the more advanced ones when I received it, but by the time it broke, it was several years old. And it was designed for everyday use—walking around the house, going to the office—rather than the heavy-duty activity I'd been subjecting it to.

Even though the final straw for that foot was just a typical daily task, by that point, I was regularly putting my prosthetic in more challenging conditions. My marathon streak was still a few years in the future, but my running journey was well underway. I'd already completed my first 50-mile ultramarathon in Umstead and run 100 miles on the treadmill. During training, I'd power hiked up to 22 miles on that foot. I'm really glad I was at home when it broke and not, say, on a run, or even at the grocery store. That would've created quite a scene!

"Well, Jacky, this just won't do," I thought. I needed to be able to walk, of course, so I grabbed my running blade. It's not that comfortable to walk on—for one thing, it doesn't have a heel, and if you think about the heel-to-toe motion of a walking stride, you can understand why that's a bit problematic. Plus, it's a bit longer than my other leg, because it has to compress more with each stride to power me forward to the next step. Wearing it when I'm *not* running feels like I'm a bit off-balance or that my hip is hiking up with every step. Still, it was better than hopping around.

Fortunately, though I was a bit shaken by the fall, the connection between my mind and my prosthetic seemed largely intact. After a wobbly first few steps, I was able to regain a rhythm to my strides.

The foot I broke had been discontinued, but I wanted to try to replace it. Most walking feet are flat or set to match one particular shoe, but the style I like is adjustable to match different pairs. That might seem like a luxury…until you try going into the women's section and finding shoes that have one specific heel height. It's nearly impossible. I'd had to push hard to get this kind of foot from the UK's National Health Service in the first place. My doctors wrote a letter saying that I, as a woman with a business career, needed it for my work. Now that I'm a professional athlete, it's not as critical for my employment, but I do like it for times when I want to wear heels or sandals. I searched around online and found the same foot on eBay, of all places. Score!

Finally, and most importantly, I made an appointment with my prosthetist to talk about getting a second type of foot, called a dynamic walking foot.

A dynamic foot is somewhat of a cross between a basic foot and a running blade. Like a blade, it's contoured and made of strong, flexible materials like carbon fiber—allowing it, like a blade, to compress and expand with every step for a smoother, more natural gait, even over bumpy ground.

However, the size and shape are tailored to the physics of walking rather than running. While my running blade is tall and arches up nearly to the bottom of my stump, giving me lots of leverage to push off when I'm running, my dynamic walking foot—the one I use is the Fillauer AllPro, though there are other brands—has a smaller C curve, with a heel jutting off the back, attached to a longer socket near where an ankle would be. This angle is better for walking, in which more of the energy comes from your foot rather than higher up the kinetic chain. Finally, there's a rubber foot shell that goes around the carbon, making it appear more like my other foot and protecting it from wear and tear, and allowing me to wear walking shoes.

Years before, when I'd gotten my first prosthetic, I wouldn't have known to ask for this type of foot. Even if I'd had an inkling of what a dynamic foot was, I may have been too afraid to speak up to request one. Now, I've learned so much more about all the available options. And, importantly, I've also gained the confidence to push for the ones that are right for me, whether that means they allow me to wear heels or run up mountains.

Doctors, physical therapists, prosthetists—most of them are very well educated and good at what they do, and the best of them will work with you to navigate complex medical systems and situations to achieve your goals. But they don't live in your body or feel what you feel. Ultimately, there's only one person who's truly best suited to know your interests and speak up for them: you.

This mindset was an evolution for me, for sure. Like many people in my generation, I was trained to think of doctors as all-knowing. And when I was thrown into the medical whirlwind of a cancer diagnosis, especially at a relatively young age, I had no choice but to rely on the expertise and guidance of my medical team. At the time I learned I had Ewing sarcoma, I was extremely fortunate to have one of the world's foremost experts on my disease right in my backyard in the Netherlands.

Edwin and I did everything we could to understand what was happening to my body and what choices, if any, I had. But things happened so fast and at such a high level, I had to let go of my sense of control and trust that the medical professionals taking care of me knew what they were doing. And they did. They saved my life. My cancer is gone, and it hasn't returned. I'm here today because of what they did for me.

When I got my first prosthetic, I was too shell-shocked and in pain to have much of an opinion on what type of foot I was receiving. The longer I lived with an amputation, though, the more I learned about what worked for me and what didn't, and the more comfortable I felt sharing that information. Getting my running blade was a crucial step forward.

At first, all I knew was that I needed something better for the sport than my walking foot, and I got the simplest, least expensive blade available. Then, mile by mile, I gained both an understanding of my body and the confidence to act on it. As I took to the trails,

I thought, "There has to be a better way. And if I work to find it for me, I know there will be others who come after me who will also benefit." I appreciate where I came from, but I'm always looking to advocate for more, for myself and other amputees.

~

The process for getting a new walking foot works like this: I go to my prosthetist and get the ball rolling. He sends me to a physical therapist, who examines me and then signs a form that says I'm still an amputee and I still need a prosthetic. I then go to another PT, where I do a series of tests that takes about forty-five minutes—things like walking in a straight line, standing on one leg, and getting my quad strength measured. They submit all this paperwork to my insurance company, which then approves or denies coverage based on the results.

While I understand the need for a formal procedure, the whole thing strikes me as a bit ridiculous to keep repeating. My leg obviously hasn't grown back. I don't walk much differently than I ever have. I'll never *not* need a prosthetic to get around. And my track record with running speaks for itself.

No insurance companies have ever completely turned down my request, although they have, at times, requested more documentation to prove I need a high-activity foot instead of a more basic one. Sometimes they'll cover only a less expensive foot and leave me to make up the difference, or they'll pay just a portion of the extra cost of the upgraded model. I'm not sure why the algorithm changes—maybe it's just a matter of who does the paperwork, or maybe, these days, it's based on keywords and artificial intelligence—but from the outside, it appears random.

And then there are the blades, which, as I mentioned, are never covered by insurance. There's not really a typical timeframe for how often you're supposed to replace them, so I have to keep my eye on how things are holding up. My prosthetist always just tells me to watch for signs of wear, like the blade feeling a bit soft, giving less bounce as I run, or appearing frayed or peeling. It's safe to say I tend to wear them down a bit more quickly than the average person. In 2024, for example, I ran 3,206 miles. Given that the median mileage for users of the popular fitness app Strava is around 420 miles per year, I'm clearly an outlier!

Although many organizations provide grants and other forms of support for people who need specialized prosthetics—Amputee Blade Runners, the Move for Jenn Foundation, Team Catapult, and the Challenged Athletes Foundation, just to name a few—the blades have been an out-of-pocket expense for me. And there, too, the process of ordering and buying is extensive, even without the need to submit documentation to my insurance company.

Both my walking foot (which locks in place with a pin) and my running blade (which sticks on with suction) start with a gel liner that slides on over my stump, and then there's a custom-fitted socket that attaches to the foot or blade. The socket must be unique to each amputee. Although we fall into two distinct groups—above-knee and below-knee—even those of us with the same number of joints can have dramatically different anatomy based on body shape and size, as well as the specifics of our trauma or surgery.

As I mentioned when I talked about trying out my first running blade, getting a socket begins with measurements and plaster molds that are used to make the test version and then the real thing. Fit is crucial. If you're using a suction system like I do, the right fit is what holds your leg on, but no matter what kind of system you use, having the right socket can help you run longer and with less pain and fatigue. Once you have a permanent socket, you can't take it back and exchange it like you would a pair of jeans you bought at the Gap.

So, when you get the test socket, it's important to give your prosthetist in-depth feedback about how it feels, so you can make changes before they produce the final version. I talked before about how tough it can be, especially at first, to distinguish between "normal" pain that comes with amputation and pain that's due to an ill-fitting socket. The more you can communicate with your prosthetist about how you're feeling—what's rubbing, pinching, chafing, or just plain not right—the better off you'll be. The more times you go through a process like this one, the more comfortable this dialogue becomes—and the more you realize you can stand up for yourself in many other situations too.

~

Any new medical situation can feel overwhelming. Whenever I meet a new amputee, I first tell them to have some grace with themselves while they're processing what's happened to them and trying to understand their next steps. Then, I advise them to start doing some research. Fortunately, there's much more information available than there used to be about the different types of prosthetics, including the pros and cons, the costs, and people's real-life experiences with them. The organizations I mentioned, such as Amputee Blade Runners and the Challenged Athletes Foundation, have extensive resources, including links to experienced prosthetists, exercises for amputee athletes, and educational opportunities, along with grants for blades and equipment.

Through those organizations, online or in real life, it's also beneficial to connect with amputees who have gone through all this before. Now that I'm frequently wearing shorts and showing my prosthetic in public, I can't tell you how many times I've been approached for advice from new amputees or their family members at a mall, grocery store, or school picnic. I'm also always connecting with other amputee runners on social media or by email; if you fall into this camp and you have a question, don't hesitate to message me!

You don't have to figure out all the answers yourself before you head into your appointments with prosthetists. That said, if you can bring some ideas of what you're hoping for and the available options, you can start the process on solid footing, so to speak. The same philosophy applies to any other medical issue and situation. I don't recommend using AI or WebMD to diagnose yourself, but spending some time reflecting on your goals and priorities when it comes to your health, as well as turning to trusted online resources or others who've gone through similar experiences, can help you prepare for any medical visit.

I find it's always helpful to remember that prosthetists—and in fact any medical professionals—are just regular people. Yes, they've gone through a lot of school and training, which makes them qualified to guide us. Unfortunately, they're also often overbooked and overburdened, and they've seen the same issues dozens or hundreds of times before, so much so that they might fall into familiar scripts and routines rather than take each detail into account.

Meanwhile, when you walk into their office, you're often processing new information and experiences, and this can make it hard to advocate for yourself. It's your life, your limb, and your health, so the whole thing is so much more personal. It's normal to feel scared and vulnerable and—especially if you have people-pleasing tendencies—like you don't want to make too much of a fuss.

But as the person who will be living in this body or wearing this prosthetic, your voice and your vote are incredibly important. Don't simply defer to someone else's opinions or tell them everything feels fine when it doesn't. Prosthetists know how to make a socket, yes, but they don't know how that socket is going to fit or function on your body unless you tell them. Doctors have the training to order and interpret lab tests, but that information is much less valuable without hearing from you about how your symptoms are affecting you.

Sometimes, all it takes is an informed question or a clearly spoken preference from a patient to snap a medical professional out of autopilot and remind them to use their skills and expertise to treat you as a whole, unique person. And you don't necessarily have to feel totally confident or sure of yourself to do it! You might even admit how you're feeling up front, saying something like, "This is all new to me and I'm feeling overwhelmed, but I know that I want to get back to the active lifestyle I had before my surgery. What solutions could help me do that?" Or, "I'm not sure how this is supposed to feel, because this is my first time through this process. My socket feels like it's pushing right on the bone, and it hurts so much I'm worried I won't be able to walk comfortably." That can flip them into problem-solving mode, making the two of you a true team with common concerns and goals.

Now, you may also find some doctors and other medical professionals who won't respond kindly, who belittle you, shame you, or insist they know better if you ask questions or verbalize your preferences. I can't emphasize enough that that's a problem with *them*, not a problem with you. When medical professionals talk down to me or ignore me, I work to find another option, looking for someone who takes me and my concerns seriously. Even if finances, insurance, or logistics make that impossible for you, I recommend that you try your best not to let anyone steamroll you. Take family members or trusted friends to appointments with you, if you can, and keep being vocal about your experiences and preferences. Even when it's tough, I find things always go better when I don't take a backseat in managing my health and well-being.

~

This advocacy isn't a one-time skill you learn—it's something you have to practice over and over. Each time I get a new running blade, there's more to the process of fine-tuning it to meet my specific physiology and the high demands I place on it. Edwin and I spent eight months and countless hours tinkering with the blade I currently run on, adjusting the settings so they feel right and move right.

I would run and he'd follow me on a bike, taking videos and watching my stride, while I monitored how I was feeling. Sometimes, I'd know something was off, and we'd then discover that my knees were knocking together or that my hips weren't aligned. We'd pause, take off my leg, then use the specialized tools that come with it to loosen a bolt or turn the foot in or out. We'd start again and repeat, until we got it right.

Once we finally found the exact settings that worked, we marked them with a permanent marker. And I'm glad we did, because each time I go back to the prosthetist's office, they try to return the blade to the factory settings. This has happened to me with nearly every prosthetic I've gotten; they do everything by the book, based on what the manufacturers recommend. But Jacky doesn't work by the book. Every time, I have to make tweaks—sometimes using settings that are essentially the opposite of what I've been told—to move comfortably and smoothly.

There isn't one solution for everyone. Sometimes you have to be stubborn until you find the one that works for you. I'm urging you, whether you're dealing with amputation or another medical situation, not to settle for less than what you want and need. You can't always fight the system, but you can take steps to make it work for you, if you stand up for yourself.

April 2024

It was another sweltering spring in Arizona. I tossed and turned, sweating, for the tenth night in a row. In the morning, I dragged myself out of bed. Running was pretty much the last thing I wanted to do—I was exhausted—but I kept up my training for the Yeti 100-miler in September as best I could.

Besides the hot flashes and sleepless nights, there was more. Despite all my mileage and no changes to my diet, I was gaining weight, especially around the middle. After the challenges of cancer, amputation, and childbirth, running had given me a way of feeling at home in my skin. Now, I was back to that bizarre feeling of disconnection, like my body wasn't mine anymore.

I told my doctor what was happening, and also that my period had stopped. To me, it was clear it all added up to perimenopause. She listened, but I didn't get the sense she took any of it too seriously. I think she felt like maybe I was just overdoing it with running and that's why I was fatigued and my cycle was off. I insisted that this wasn't normal for me. And because I was confident about what I was feeling and what I wanted, she started to listen and ordered bloodwork to see what was going on.

As I waited for results, I was doing what I usually do: looking for information and support, online and among friends. Jeannette, my running friend from North Carolina, was about the same age and was having similar symptoms. Our stories echoed each other's. We just weren't feeling like ourselves, and our doctors weren't taking us seriously. Knowing someone else was going through it too made it feel at least a bit more bearable; we might not have had the answers, but we validated each other's experiences. In a moment of vulnerability, I posted on Instagram too, explaining I was perimenopausal, describing my symptoms, and saying I was looking for support and ideas.

The community came through, and I got both. Among the resources people suggested were books by scientist Stacy Sims; the Feisty Menopause community of athletes, led by Stacy's coauthor and the badass endurance athlete Selene Yeager; and, above all, hormone replacement therapy (HRT). Woman after woman posted that, even if they were somewhat reluctant to take it at first, HRT wound up being a game-changer for them.

When I got my blood test results back, my usual doctor was on holiday, so my file was transferred to another doctor. When I went in for my appointment, he was incredibly dismissive. "No, that's not anything to do with perimenopause or menopause," he said. "Look at these levels—your thyroid hormones are off. You need to start taking thyroid medication right now."

Now, that didn't sound right to me at all. My mom and my brother both have thyroid issues, so I know my results often look a bit wonky. I wanted at least one more test to make sure of what was happening before I started a medication I knew I would have to take for the rest of my life. I tried to explain all this to him, but he simply wouldn't listen, insisting his opinion was the right one. So, I told him I'd wait until my usual doctor returned, thank you very much.

When she did, she ordered more tests. "Your thyroid is absolutely fine," she told me when the lab results came back. "It's not that at all. You're definitely in perimenopause."

We talked about treatments, and knowing how much it had helped others, I asked specifically about HRT. She prescribed it, and while I can't say it was a magic fix for everything, it's been incredibly helpful. I no longer have hot flashes, my weight has shifted down and stabilized, and I can sleep through the night again, most of the time. If you're a woman in this stage of life, your experience may be different—definitely work with your own doctor on the best ways to manage your symptoms and protect your health—but I know this was the right call for me.

I was furious at the other doctor, but so glad I waited to get a second opinion. My whole prosthetic journey had taught me to stand up for myself. I wasn't going to let someone else shut me down or tell me that what I was experiencing in my body wasn't valid. I'm not saying to ignore your doctors or turn away from modern medicine. But if they're not listening to you, or if your gut tells you that something about their advice is off, don't be afraid to ask questions, say what you mean, and seek a second opinion. You know your body best, and in the end, you're the person living with it. I also firmly believe that if more of us advocate for ourselves in this way, we'll continue to change the culture in such a way that means amputees, women, and everyone else will get the type of medical care they need and deserve in the future.

DON'T BE AFRAID TO CRY

Marathon 72 of 104

"What am I doing? Why am I out here? Whose stupid idea was this anyway?"

The sand felt gritty under my hands as I sat on the side of the trail. There was absolutely nothing wrong with my leg or my stump. My brain, however, was a different story. On mile 15 of day 72, more than 1,900 miles into the challenge, it had entered full meltdown mode, convinced this entire adventure was worthless.

"What made you think you could do this? And why would you even want to? You've done a lot of dumb things, but this might just be the dumbest yet." The inner voice I was hearing was loud, and it wanted me not only to quit but also to feel bad about ever having started.

Sitting in the shadow of a saguaro, I cried. Big, ugly tears dripped into the dust as I became convinced I couldn't go another step.

Yet there I was, in the middle of my typical 1.6-mile loop at Veterans Oasis Park. If nothing else, I'd have to shuffle back to my car somehow.

So, I took a deep breath and brought myself back to the present moment. I did a mental scan of my body, noticing that I was fatigued but not hurting—at least, not any more than could be expected after 72 marathons in the previous 71 days. "You can do hard things, Jacky," I told myself. "It's normal that you're tired. This challenge is tough—but you have very good reasons for taking it on."

That led me to consider my "why." I called to mind all the people who'd sent me messages saying I inspired them to start running or to do something else they'd doubted they could. I pictured my kids and how they'd ask after me when I got home ("Mummy, have you done your marathon yet?"). Most of all, I thought of the Jacky who had the courage to start this journey in the first place, unsure of just how far she could take it.

I stood up, dusted myself off, and lifted my head. "Let's just get to the next mile," I said. When I got there, I threw myself a little celebration, literally raising my hands in the air and cheering for myself. Then, I thought, "Just one mile more." I passed the parking lot—and kept going, until, eventually, the whole 26.2 was done.

~

In an instant, I'm a kid again. My brother, Lionel, and I, barely kindergarten age, are peering at each other under the table as adults laugh and glasses clink overhead. We knew children technically weren't supposed to be in the pub. Our parents, who'd brought us here for their usual night of carousing, shushed us whenever we dared to speak or poke our heads out to ask for another cup of Fanta.

Even in more child-friendly situations—visiting our grandmother's house, at the grocery store, around the dinner table—we were urged to be seen but not heard. When we did talk, we most definitely never discussed anything as squishy as feelings. If we cried or yelled, we were likely to be punished as a result. That was especially true for me, as the girl, who was supposed to be "perfect." I started to absorb the lesson that having feelings wasn't right and that being sad or angry made me a terrible person. Whenever I had a down day, a problem at school, or a disagreement with a friend, I figured it out on my own, stuffing my feelings deep inside so my parents wouldn't detect them. Eventually, I'd go numb.

Perhaps that's one reason why, when I got cancer years later, I wasn't inclined to speak up about how it was affecting me. As I mentioned, there wasn't much talk about mental health at the time; doctors never discussed the topic of how a brush with death or the amputation necessary to avert it might affect someone psychologically. Every checkup focused only on how my prosthetic was fitting or how the wounds on my leg were healing, not how I was coping with the fear and loss. And there was just so much to do—follow-up appointments, learning to walk again, and going back to work at the office, which I did just six weeks after surgery. I had enough pain to deal with already; I didn't need the added distraction of uncomfortable emotions. If I could keep charging forward instead, maybe I would wake up from this dream and get back to real life.

It wasn't until several months later that the full weight of the grief hit me. This isn't an uncommon experience when someone goes through a major medical event or other trauma. Research shows that secondary psychological effects, such as post-traumatic stress disorder and depression, can occur months to years later. In the beginning, you're just trying to make it through. But over time, those buried feelings demand to be heard, growing until you can't ignore them any longer.

At first, I was hesitant to give in to my feelings of sorrow and loss. Who was I to complain about my amputation? I had survived cancer, after all! Plus, the outside world praised me for keeping a positive attitude and recovering quickly. My doctors—and Edwin's parents, who'd come to stay with us after surgery—kept commenting on how well I was doing. My office even gave me a "Passion for Winning" award. The recognition was lovely and thoughtful, but it also made me feel like others expected a lot of me.

Guilt and shame surrounded every less-than-perfect day. I would cry, then feel like I was letting people down for being upset. My anger would bubble up—I can't tell you how many times I tossed my crutches across the room in frustration—and then shame would wash over me, as if being upset were another sign of weakness.

Eventually, I got to a breaking point. Edwin could sense the shift: I cried more, I stayed in bed longer, I ate less. He added up all the warning signs and realized I was entering a full-blown depression.

"Jacky, they didn't clip your toenails. They amputated your leg," he said. "It's like losing someone close to you. You need to grieve."

Hearing those words helped me see that he was right. I couldn't keep pushing these feelings down or they'd consume me. I had to fall apart, to truly feel and acknowledge the difficult parts, before I could begin moving forward and healing.

~

Emotions exist for a reason. They're like messages from our mind to our body, giving us signals about our needs and driving us to act on them. They also connect to others us through a shared sense of vulnerability and empathy; the more intense the emotions you experience with another person, the deeper your bond.

In order to build those connections and translate emotions into insights and actions, though, we first have to truly feel them—even the not-so-fun ones, such as sadness, fear, and grief.

It's normal to want to turn away or shut down when things hurt. However, as my cancer experience taught me, denying your grief only makes it deeper and isolates you further. When I charged forward as if my sadness and loss didn't exist, they kept growing deep inside me, until they had no choice but to burst out.

It's also all too easy to get hooked in feelings about your feelings—that layer of guilt and shame that comes when our sadness or anger starts to break through. We tell ourselves that we don't deserve to feel bad, that others have it worse, or that people expect us to buck up and power through. We're beating ourselves up for being humans, telling ourselves, "You're overreacting" or "No one cares what you really feel." Besides distracting us from the messages our emotions are sending, these feelings about our feelings usually make our mood even worse. Negative self-talk contributes to a downward spiral, where all those layers of yuck keep building and churning until they nearly consume us.

I've always found it helpful to take a step back and imagine what I would tell a friend who was hurting. I wouldn't tell them they were being dramatic or that others have it worse. Instead, I'd hug them and listen as they shared what they were going through. Then, I'd offer words of assurance: "It's okay that you're feeling this way." "I know it's tough, but I'm here for you." "I believe you can get through this."

Contrary to the way I was brought up, or to anyone who views crying as a weakness, there's tremendous power in connecting with your feelings, including the bad ones. Once you acknowledge what it is you're going through, to others or even just to yourself, you may feel an almost instant surge of relief. Our emotions are sometimes like little kids squirming in their seats in class, dying for someone to notice them. Once you turn their way and call their name, they often calm down on their own.

I've learned, through the years, to have what I call a pity party, a time when I wallow for a while in despair or let myself seethe with rage. I let the feelings wash over me, without judging myself for having them. The length and intensity depend on where I am and what it is I'm coping with. Sometimes it's just a few minutes during a race to gather my thoughts and keep moving. In other cases, such as when I'm dealing with an injury that makes me miss a race, I need a day or two (or more) to mourn.

When you throw a pity party, no emotion is off limits. You can feel angry at yourself or your situation, betrayed by your body or by someone in your life, frustrated at your limitations, or overwhelmed by the circumstances you're facing. Sometimes you need to yell and scream or throw something, which is totally okay, as long as you don't hurt anyone else! The key is to know when it's time to shut down the pity party, sending your guests (misery, rage, etc.) on their way.

Some of this happens naturally. Once you've acknowledged these feelings, they often start to shrink down to a more manageable size. It's almost like riding a wave: Your emotions rise as you pay attention to them, then begin to subside once you stop fighting them.

From there, you can take active steps to pick yourself up and pull yourself forward. Once my rage or sadness has retreated from its peak, I can often coach myself through the rest with compassion and positive self-talk, just like I would that theoretical friend. "This is hard, Jacky, but you can do it," I say, out loud. "It's true that you're missing a leg now. You have to accept that. But it hasn't held you back. Look at all you have and what you've accomplished." "Just show up and do your best. It will always be enough."

~

Often, once we've allowed them in, we can see that our emotions point us toward actions we can take to fulfill our needs. If we realize we're feeling alone and abandoned, for instance, we can ask for more support. When we're overwhelmed and exhausted, it's a clear sign we could benefit from rest. Think back to my experience at Across the Years and the power of a nap to ward off grumpiness and restore equilibrium. It's sort of incredible, when you think about it: Our feelings act almost as trail markers, guiding us along the path to greater well-being.

In my mind, it's like doing a post-race analysis, going back through what went well and what didn't, to gain lessons for the next time. For example, when I attempted the Umstead 100, in 2021, I made it to 65 miles before I missed a pacing cutoff and had to stop. I was gutted, but once I gave myself time to sit in disappointment for a bit, I went back through and realized there was so much I could take away from the experience.

Heavy rain had gotten into my socket, loosening the suction and causing friction that pulled the skin right off my stump. I'd learned that, in the future, I'd look for a different and more waterproof valve. Edwin was my crew, pacer, and childcare coordinator, but we learned that there was no way one person could make sure I was eating enough, check my skin, pace me, *and* ensure two kids didn't run off into the forest. Next time, I knew, I'd need to recruit a bigger team.

Doing this kind of debriefing of our emotional life requires us to get in touch with our feelings, to observe them as if they were data from our GPS watch, rather than fear them as if they were threats to avoid. We need both full-blown pity parties and moments of reflection—sitting down in the dirt with our sadness, letting the tears fall when they need to, and maybe talking it through with someone we trust. That might be a close friend, a family member, or a mental health professional. If you're really in the thick of a tough time or dark thoughts, I encourage you to reach out to someone trained to give you support.

I've done all this myself. Hitting the low point after my surgery and recovery, I learned to give myself more grace and to stop fighting reality. With time and patience, I climbed out of the hole. Still, every so often, those low feelings return. After both of my kids were born, for instance, I found myself once again coping with feelings of worthlessness, not belonging, and even wondering what the point of it all was.

Those feelings of sadness and futility were quickly followed by intense waves of guilt and shame. I'd see other mothers instantly bond with their children, saying how natural the whole process felt, and meanwhile, I felt like a failure because I was struggling. Was I a terrible mom? Did I just not love my kids? Why wasn't any of it enough? Why wasn't *I* enough? Deep down, I also harbored another fear. My mother had been diagnosed with bipolar disorder when I was young, and life with her was far from easy. I worried that I—and my kids—were doomed to follow a similar path.

I was in enough of a downward spiral after Dexter was born that I realized I couldn't fix it all by myself. I got my courage up and talked to my doctor. Saying the words "I'm struggling" out loud wasn't easy, especially the first time. To my surprise, the doctor was extremely kind and quickly got me the help I needed for what I would come to learn was postpartum depression. Hearing that there was a name for what I was experiencing, and that it wasn't my fault or something I could control, was validating. I went on antidepressants until my hormones and mood stabilized and I could wean myself off. For me, that was the right decision. The medication made me feel much more like myself again, and the point came when I no longer needed it…that is, until after Eliza was born, when I had similar feelings.

This time around, things were even more challenging because I was also caring for a toddler. Fortunately, I spotted the warning signs a little earlier, speaking up before I sank quite as low. Once again, I worked with my doctor on a plan, one that involved medication for the short term.

Despite what I felt at first, I now know there's zero shame in any of this; treatment is available for postpartum depression and every other mental health condition. If you're in a crisis, especially if you're thinking about hurting yourself or someone else, you can dial 988 for help; otherwise, your primary care doctor is a great place to start. Therapists, counselors, and support groups can play a key role too.

Coping with these feelings isn't easy. Delving into them and trying to decode what they're telling you doesn't always feel great, especially at first. Asking for support can feel like the hardest step of all. But as you practice connecting to your emotions, it gets easier, and you'll realize how much better you feel afterward. To me, it's like training for a race. The more time you spend doing the hard work, the more resilient an athlete—and human—you'll be when it counts.

August 2019

I stepped off the track, deflated and discouraged. It was Saturday, and I was supposed to run 12 miles around the oval as part of my buildup for the Kansas City Marathon, a race I had been invited to run by one of my sponsors, Garmin. But the mental challenge of so many small loops had gotten to me, and I sank into the grass in defeat after only 6 miles.

I would have much preferred to be out on the trails. I'd finished the TransRockies stage race a couple of weeks prior, and my heart was still back there in the mountains. But after returning home, I discovered there was a problem with the valve on my prosthetic. My prosthetist, Chandler, figured that it had something to do with the altitude in the Rockies, as maybe the change in air pressure at elevation had disrupted the delicate balance that forms the suction needed to keep my leg on. That suction was so unstable that any change in terrain knocked it loose, causing my leg to fall off and me to hit the ground—ouch!

Until the new valve he ordered for me came in, the track or treadmill were my only safe choices. At that point, I hadn't quite developed the mental muscle to cope with the monotony of tiny loops for more than 48 laps, as I would during the marathon challenge. Besides, I hated that I was in this position in the first place. It was one of those times when I found being an amputee incredibly frustrating. "Why can't I just run like everyone else?" I thought. "This is so unfair." There on the ground by the track, I lowered my head into my hands, a pity party underway.

Two important things happened the next day. First, once those feelings of frustration and anger were out of my system, I was able to head back to the track and finish the other half of my workout. Then, I noticed that Edwin had taken a photo of me slumped over in the grass. We always worked together to document my life as a runner, but I usually only posted the positive things—the finish lines, the new personal bests, the signs of progress. Since he captured this low moment, though, I decided to go ahead and make that public as well.

In my opinion, social media has often made it even harder to connect with our emotions and let go of those "feelings about feelings" on top of them. When I started getting into running, I found other athletes' posts purely inspiring. When I encountered some of the harder moments in my own journey, though, I felt a disconnect. None of the other runners I followed ever seemed to have struggles or doubts. I wondered if I was alone in these challenges. I started judging my worst days against only their filtered, positive posts. Meanwhile, every once in a while, someone would say something to me that had me worrying about my own role in the cycle. I'd hear, "You make it look so easy!" and realize I wasn't letting anyone else in on the harder parts of my process either.

So by posting the photo of my breakdown on the grass, I decided I wanted to be part of the solution rather than add to the problem. I wrote a caption about what I was struggling with, including how my blade issues were keeping me from pursuing my goals in the way I would like and how frustrated I was by the lack of control I felt. "Running can be really hard," I confessed. "It's definitely not all sunshine and roses." I worried a little bit about showing so much vulnerability, wondering what people would think of me as an athlete. Still, I took a deep breath and pushed "post" anyway.

The response made it clear I'd hit on something. In the comments, others were sharing their own struggles, the mental and physical hurdles that stood between them and the sport they loved. "Running has been hard for me this week too," one person wrote. "I just wasn't 'feeling it' this Saturday either," said another. A third: "I so appreciate your honesty, since we too often share the successes and not often enough the struggle."

In fact, the more I talked openly—on social media and elsewhere—about the challenges I was facing, both in running and outside of it, the more I recognized how universal they were. And recently, more athletes than ever write and speak about the bad days as well as the good ones. While running and other physical activities are powerful mood boosters, they're also hard sports with their own difficulties, and they don't make us immune to depression, anxiety, or other mental conditions.

I now make it a regular habit to post not only when I accomplish something big but also when I fall short, or when I am feeling so down I don't even want to try. And when I'm interviewed on a podcast or I meet people in person, I don't shy away from discussions about mental health. Through these conversations, it's become even clearer to me that emotional vulnerability bonds us.

Talking with others about the dark moments lets a bit of light in through the cracks. It's as if we're all running at night wearing headlamps; sometimes, your battery can drain and leave you stranded in the blackness. If we run together, sharing the glow of the beams that remain, we can make it through to the morning.

~

When something bad happens to us—whether it's a cancer diagnosis, a running injury, or the loss of someone or something we love—it can shake our fundamental beliefs about ourselves and the world. Why is this happening to us? How could the fates—or God, or whichever force you believe organizes the universe—be so cruel? Does this mean we aren't the strong athletes or humans we presumed that we were?

After my amputation, I asked, again and again, "Why me? What did I do to deserve this?" When I didn't get an answer—not from my doctors, not from Edwin, and certainly not from any kind of higher power—I gave up, for a while. I buried myself in the business of living and did my best to put the past behind me, rejecting labels like "amputee," "disabled," and even "survivor."

Finding running finally gave me the courage to open that box again, to make sense of all I'd been through, and to write a new ending to my story. Again, I'm not a religious person. I don't necessarily believe everything happens for a reason. But reflecting on all that's occurred since my first 5K has made me realize that there is so much good that's come out of my challenges.

Without my losses, I wouldn't have learned to stand up for myself, or to teach other amputees to do so for themselves. If so many people hadn't discouraged me from running as an amputee, I might not have been so determined to start—and to persevere, even when it got tough. I wouldn't have had the privilege of climbing mountains or setting records or running quiet, peaceful miles on the trails with my husband or my kids.

I'd be an entirely different person, and although I'm sure she would have been great, gosh do I love the badass female athlete I've become. And an entirely different person likely wouldn't be here right now telling you my story, bonding us together in a way that's incredibly healing.

None of this means I don't still have bad days and dark moments. There are times when the pressure of performing in public gets to me and I need to take a few beats to step back and sit in the quiet. Other times, depression comes out of the blue and knocks me down for no discernible reason. The difference is that, now, I can recognize it, realize what I need to do to bring myself out of it, and trust that I'll get through it.

~

Marathon 72 of 104

The more you run marathons and ultramarathons, the more you learn about the incredible resilience of the human mind and body. One of the things that has surprised me the most is how the whole roller coaster of physical sensations and emotions can repeat, over and over, during the same race. You can go from feeling like you're flying in one mile to dragging and fatigued the next, and then suddenly getting a new burst of energy and optimism. Yes, sometimes a race starts poorly and continues that way, but just as often, if you can manage to navigate the rough patches, you'll start feeling better again on the other side.

When I finally did finish marathon 72, I felt simultaneously depleted and triumphant. I went home that night and did my usual recovery ritual—getting in a post-run recovery snack and then a nutritious dinner, taking an Epsom salt bath, and using a massage gun on my right leg and especially my stump. I tried not to think about what I was going to feel like in the morning. If you'd asked for my prediction, I would have said I would probably struggle, again.

The next morning, though, I woke up surprisingly refreshed. I got up, got the kids off to school, and headed out the door. I took one running step, then another, then another—and was shocked to find that I felt strong, mentally and physically. Truly, I realized, I'm capable of so much more than I ever thought possible.

10

WALK IF YOU HAVE TO

Marathon 83 of 104

By marathon 83, I thought I'd figured out how to handle Arizona's brutal heat. I was wrong.

Things started out smoothly enough. "It's a really nice morning! I'm feeling so good," I said to my friend and fellow ultrarunner Rachel Belmont. She nodded, her black cap bobbing up and down in agreement.

This was a Saturday, April 9. I was grateful that Rachel was free to meet up. Although Eliza, nine, sometimes ran a few of my miles with me on the weekends, I'd done most of my marathons alone.

Rachel had been following me online for several years, and eventually we connected in real life. She's a true adventurer—she loves jumping out of planes, as well as running through deserts—so although she's based in Phoenix, our schedules don't always align. But when we do have the chance to run together, we swap stories of everything from the most far-flung races to our favorite movies.

And I was extra glad to have her company on this day. As the miles ticked by, the temperature steadily rose. By mile 12, as the mercury inched toward 100°F, I could feel my energy seeping away, like water poured into the desert sand. My skin prickled and my breathing grew heavier as the heat started to overtake me.

"Okay, maybe I'm actually not feeling so great after all," I told Rachel.

I slowed to a walk. Rachel nodded again and fell in stride beside me. "You've got this, Jacky," she said. "Just keep persisting."

I did, and we walked along, our chatter fell mostly silent as I concentrated on my effort. From time to time, she'd offer another few words of encouragement: "You're a superhuman." "You've done it all—you can do this too." "The whole running community is so proud of you."

It took us nearly seven hours, but we eventually hit the 26.2-mile mark. At the end, I was crusted in salt, but we shared a sweaty hug. It didn't matter to me how long it took or whether we ran the whole way. The goal was to keep moving, to finish, and to celebrate.

October 2020

Pilot Mountain to Hanging Rock. Even the names sound intimidating. As I made my way along the 50-kilometer journey between these two North Carolina peaks—one that ascends more than 4,000 feet across those 31 miles—I found out the race was indeed a bit fearsome.

In October 2020, racing opportunities were still scarce due to COVID-19 restrictions. The only events I'd been able to do since March were virtual ones. When I found out this race was taking place as planned, I jumped at the chance to take part. Edwin had done the 50-miler here a few years prior, in 2018, so I had a pretty good idea of what to expect—several stream crossings, long climbs up and down trails covered in rocks and roots, and aid stations stocked with peanut butter Rice Krispies treats. Yum!

The race was about a two-hour drive from home, in Pinnacle, North Carolina, so we stayed overnight near the start. It had rained some the day before, and I was a bit concerned about the weather. When my early-morning alarm woke me, in time to catch the 6:00 a.m. shuttle to the starting line, it was already starting to sprinkle. "Just my luck," I thought, my mind flashing back to the muddy mess of my first ultra at Triple Lakes.

Right about the time the race kicked off at 7:45, the downpour began. I did my best to navigate the roots and switchbacks, staring hard at the trail to avoid slipping. As I started into the first big climb around mile 8, I took a step and—squelch!—I hit the mud, my blade going one direction and my leg another.

I got back up and straightened myself out. Nothing was cut or broken, but with each step, my stump throbbed like a twisted ankle. I gutted out the next 4 miles, slowly, to around the 12-mile mark, where Edwin was waiting.

I arrived there disappointed in the way my race was going. I wasn't sure it was wise to continue, given the amount of pain I was already enduring. But stubborn as I am, I didn't want to quit if I didn't have to.

When I saw Edwin, I had an idea. He had my walking foot—that new dynamic AllPro—in case I did decide to call it quits. What if I could put it on and keep going?

When I was only running on the roads, the idea of switching legs to walk during a race would have seemed outrageous to me. Runners *run*, after all. However, back when I was training for my first 50-miler, I got a critical piece of advice from another athlete. "If you want to be a stronger ultrarunner, you need to learn to hike faster," he told me. Although the sport is called "ultrarunning," no one makes it through 200 or 400 miles without at least some time walking, especially when the course is technical.

I took this advice to heart and began adding long power walks to my training weeks. I didn't stress at all if I had to go slowly up a steep incline, or bum-shuffle down it, during a race. But I still hesitated to walk on flat sections, for reasons that were equal parts ego and logistics. To my mind, putting on a walking foot essentially would have meant accepting defeat, and my previous model of walking foot—the one that had broken on me in the kitchen—wasn't made for long distances or tricky terrain.

Today, though, the equation felt different to me. The AllPro foot just might be up to the challenge of a long-distance hike in the Sauratown Mountains, I realized. Plus, it has a whole other type of system—the pin lock versus the suction of my blade—and it would put pressure on a different part of my stump, potentially easing the pain I was feeling. I was also further absorbing the mentality of the trail, which is to use the best equipment for the challenge at hand.

As Edwin stood by with extra fluids and snacks, I switched from my blade to my foot. I stood up and took a few hesitant steps forward. "Whew," I said with a sense of relief. "That feels so, so much better."

I forged ahead, striding down the rest of the first mountain and up and down the second one. I mostly walked, running a little, but not so much that the pin socket would irritate my stump. It might have taken me eleven hours to reach the finish line, but pace wasn't my priority. Without the change in tactics and equipment, I never would have gotten there at all.

~

That race cemented a lesson I've learned many times: slow and steady sometimes really does win the race. Like I've said before, forward is forward. In a world that urges us to push full speed ahead, it's not always easy to back off. However, changing your gait just might be the thing that makes the impossible possible again. Now, my race plans almost always involve bringing my walking foot and knowing that, at some point, switching to it will be the right decision to get me to the finish line. And in the spring of 2025, I also learned that sometimes the longer path is the best route.

While most races involve a carefully measured course, the Speed Project is another animal entirely. Since 2013, relay teams of runners have traveled the approximately 300 miles between Los Angeles and Las Vegas in an invitation-only event that's the brainchild of Nils Arend, a German runner who once organized raves.

True to Nils's background, the Speed Project's vibe is reminiscent of an underground dance party. It's unsanctioned—meaning he doesn't request permits or close off roads like, say, the organizer of a big-city marathon would—and you don't sign up on a website; you have to contact Nils on WhatsApp and plead your case for an entry. The race slogan is "No rules, no spectators," and there are also no aid stations and no corporate sponsors. Each team maps its own path through the cities and deserts of the Southwest. Shortcuts are not only allowed, they're encouraged, provided you're brave enough to forge a new path.

A solo option was added a few years ago, giving individual runners the chance to test their grit and endurance. When I first heard about it from some runners who'd participated a few years before, I felt that familiar pull, the simultaneous sense of wonder, excitement, and fear that lets me know I have a new mission. No other amputee had made the journey. But if anyone could, I wanted it to be me.

I hunted down Nils's information and made my pitch. After an extensive interview process, he agreed.

That's how I found myself standing at the Santa Monica Pier at 4:00 a.m. on a March morning. It was me and forty other solo runners—about half of us women, which was a huge focus for the race this year—plus a crowd of crew members and supporters. Even though we'd just met in person for the first time, it already felt like a bit of a reunion. For months leading up to the race, we'd had regular Zoom calls both for all the solo runners and for just the women specifically. In between, we chatted on WhatsApp, trading maps, packing tips, safety advice, and words of encouragement.

Now, finally, it was go time. It's safe to say this wasn't your typical starting line. Under the glow of the pier's neon lights, Jarick Walker—a former football player turned runner who works as the race's brand director and host—led the crowd through a rousing call-and-response chant that ended with a countdown. We all started running, then scattered as we followed our separate routes into the city streets and beyond.

~

My original plan was to run unsupported, carrying everything I needed—including my walking foot. I'd buy extra food and supplies along the way, I figured. Edwin and the kids drove the 400-ish miles from Gilbert to Los Angeles to see me off, but Dexter and Eliza had testing at school beginning on Tuesday, so they had to return home and couldn't stay to crew me.

I'd mapped out a 289-mile route, aiming to finish in six days, and I booked hotel rooms along the way. I knew, both from the race manual and conversations with other solo runners, that there were places a woman shouldn't run alone at night, so I planned to move during the day and rest my head in a safe place when the sun went down.

The night before the race, though, my plans changed. My brother,

Lionel, who lives in Yosemite, called Edwin. "I don't feel comfortable with her doing this on her own," he said. "I'm going to come out." So he steered his big black Ford truck down to meet me the first day of my journey.

I'd plugged my route into my Garmin GPS watch, so all I had to do was follow the directions it gave me. I kept my pace relaxed as the sun rose over the palm trees and I ran down the sidewalk. Hours passed, and I found myself amazed at how far I could go and still be within Los Angeles city limits. It didn't help that I kept having to stop for what felt like the world's longest traffic lights—an annoying obstacle I wasn't expecting!

Within the span of a few blocks, I traveled from a part of town where people slept on the street to one filled with mega-mansions and gated communities. LA has a reputation for being superficial and snooty, but I found pedestrians of every type to be friendly and welcoming; I paused often to answer questions about my prosthetic. When the sun got a little too bright and hot, I ducked into a McDonald's and ordered a frozen Coca-Cola, sitting in the air conditioning and savoring every sip.

Lionel and I connected in a parking lot after I'd run about 49 miles. The heat had sapped me more than I expected, and the sun had long since gone down. I took a nap in the back of his pickup. When I woke up, we strategized about the next section of the route.

While flying completely solo would have been challenging in many ways, having a crew at an event like this requires planning and coordination. Lionel had only been to one of my races, the Moab 240, so this type of adventure was new to him. We decided that, most of the time, it made far more sense for him to go ahead and wait for me than to follow behind me. And there were places I would run—trails in the Mojave Desert, for instance—where he couldn't drive. This meant a bit of guesswork on timing to coordinate when and where to meet up.

Some runners and teams have detailed spreadsheets, but again, that's not exactly how I work. I showed him the map I'd be following, and we identified the next few connection points, promising to keep in touch by phone if things changed or if one of us sensed danger.

As it turned out, I was grateful that I didn't have to carry my extra foot with me the whole time. When you're trekking through the desert in 90°F heat, a spare prosthetic feels quite heavy! But that also meant I had less flexibility in swapping out equipment. I wanted to go back and forth between my foot and my blade to vary the pressure on my stump, but I had to wait for each meetup with Lionel to do so.

Midway through day 2, I was feeling good. Since I'd been moving a bit more slowly than planned, I was itching to pick up the pace and make up some time. I was about 3 miles out from meeting Lionel when I thought, "I just need to go!" and broke into a run while wearing my walking foot.

In retrospect, it was such a rookie move. Though that walking foot is lighter and more dynamic than my original one—I didn't *quite* feel like I was dragging a load of bricks—it still isn't designed to bear the impact of pounding against the ground that happens when I attempt even the slowest jog. The force shoots up my stump, and the pin lock that connects to my leg bumps right up against my bare skin.

When I reached Lionel, I was still feeling okay...or so I thought. But when I took off my walking foot to put on my blade, I realized I was in trouble. The slamming of the pin lock against my stump had bruised my stump badly. I could barely even touch it, and when I tried to put on my running blade, the pain was immense.

From that point on, the most I could manage on my blade was about 3 miles at a time, and at a pace that felt glacial despite the desert heat. "This is ridiculous," I told Lionel, as he stopped the truck in yet another gas station parking lot. "My brain and my body just aren't connected right now. It's frustrating, because I just want to go, but my body's not allowing me." My ego wanted me to run, but I was slower on the blade than I was when I hiked with my walking foot. And then there was all the time and agony required to switch back and forth.

When my stump swells up, which it continued to do throughout that journey, even putting my walking foot on is a huge challenge. The silicon sleeve that I roll on doesn't fit properly, with the pin shifted to the side rather than straight on the bottom. That means it doesn't align with the hole in the prosthetic, and I don't hear the satisfying "click" that lets me know I'm safe to put my weight on it.

Instead, I have to continue shifting the liner and trying to shove it into the leg, jumping and stamping. This took me as long as half an hour—and it hurt like hell.

So, the plan changed, again. I put my blade on and jogged a bit every once in a while, but mostly, I walked. I trashed the schedule I'd projected and instead took it one meetup at a time. With a truck and my brother to help me stay safe, I could sleep when I needed, usually two to four hours at a time. But mostly, I kept moving.

~

And oh, the things I saw along the way. At a power-walking pace, I didn't have to stare down at the ground the whole time, watching my footing. I absorbed far more of the world around me than I otherwise would have—the palm trees turning into the oaks and pines of the national forest, then giving way to desert shrubs; the lizards skittering away; the rose-gold sunrises and sunsets. I think everyone should have an experience like this, where it's just you and the open road for hours on end.

Despite my sleep deprivation, my senses seemed ultra-heightened. Perhaps it was a survival mechanism, but I swear I could see every star in the sky, hear the tiniest creature rustle in the underbrush, and smell fast-food restaurants miles away. In some sections, this paid off in keeping me safe.

The third day was eerily foggy, and as trains rumbled by in the distance, the heavy mist sat right above the road. Despite my bright-orange jacket and lighted vest, drivers couldn't see me on the roadside. I learned to move aside quickly when I heard the low hum of tires approaching, so I didn't wind up as roadkill.

My instincts, too, seemed sharper than normal. For that, I was grateful. At one point, not far from the California town of Barstow, I passed a house with three fierce-looking pit bulls in the front yard. Two of them stood and barked at me from behind a tall fence, but I noticed that the third darted around the back, and I instantly felt uneasy. Sure enough, he'd found a way out of the yard and was soon barreling toward me.

My heart pounded. Time seemed to move in slow motion. I debated hitting him with one of my trekking poles, but I worried I'd just make him angrier, and potentially break my pole in the process. So I pulled out the pepper spray I'd brought to protect against any kind of predator—human or animal—and held it in front of me.

I felt awful. I have three dogs myself and didn't want to hurt him! However, his job was to protect his property, and he viewed me as a threat. It was him or me. As he leapt toward me, I pushed down hard on the spray button, aiming for his face.

To my surprise, he didn't bark or whimper or cry. He stopped in his tracks and shook his head, looking bewildered. The steps I took as I bolted away may have been my fastest ones all week!

Later, from a safe distance, I opened WhatsApp to give other runners a heads-up. We'd been posting updates in two groups—one for all the solo runners, and one with just women—warning each other about blocked roads, animals, and similar hazards. If someone was in trouble or separated from their crew, others stepped up to find them and bring them fuel and water. After the start, I only saw other runners occasionally, such as during one beautiful moment on the second day, when several of us connected, hugged, and ran together for a bit. But even when we were miles apart, the text chains formed a virtual network to get us all through.

~

Now, about that longer route. One reason I added mileage to the 289 I'd planned is because of wise advice from the group. Originally, I'd planned to run all 95 miles of Powerline Road, a popular shortcut for Speed Project racers that stretches from Barstow, California, to

Primm, Nevada. It's a service road that lies between transmission towers, which is where it gets the name, and it's highly technical, alternating between sand and rocky gravel. That type of surface is tough for me on a good day. With my compromised stump, I was in agony.

The last section was especially gnarly, with rough rocks only four-wheel-drive could handle. Fortunately, another solo runner had my back. She recommended that I take a smoother route, albeit one with more elevation. In addition to the hills, it added several miles to my total, but it was much easier going, bruises and all.

A bit more added mileage came after another of the most heart-pumping moments of the journey. It was around 1:00 a.m., and I was on the road not far from Victorville, California. The race manual specifically mentioned that this wasn't a place to leave female runners on their own, thanks to the nearby prison and a notoriously high crime rate. Because of that, and the late hour, Lionel was driving along slightly behind me as I shuffled forward in the glare of his headlights.

For miles, there was no one besides us, only darkness. Then, suddenly, three police vehicles arrived. One officer, a woman, pulled up in front of me and stopped her car sideways across my path to halt me.

I stood, shaking, and dropped my poles to the ground. My mind reeled. Had I "run" a red light I wasn't supposed to? Was I in trouble because the race was unsanctioned? I'm sure I looked equal parts exhausted and terrified as she got out of the car and walked toward me.

"Wha-what did I do?" I stammered.

"Oh—you're not in trouble, at least not from us," she said. "We got a report of suspicious behavior. Someone called and said a woman was walking alone on the road, with a man following her. We're here to see if you're okay. Are you?"

I exhaled with relief and motioned to Lionel to come over. "Yes, it's all right," I said. "He's my brother." I explained what we were doing—vaguely, so as not to get the race organizers in trouble—and assured them he was there to look out for me.

By this time, the other officers had also approached. They listened with curiosity. "Wait, you're going all the way to Vegas?" one said.

"Yeah, just 185 miles to go!" I joked.

"Well, you probably really don't want to be going this way," he replied. "I wouldn't be out here by myself." He pulled up his map and suggested I veer off old Route 66 and go around the town, rather than straight through it. I could see that it would take me yet farther out of the way, up a steep incline.

But when a cop tells you a place is sketchy, you're wise to listen. I was already a day behind schedule; what was a few more miles in the big picture? Lionel and I made the turn.

Funny enough, two other people stopped us after that, asking after me to make sure I wasn't being harassed or chased. Despite the dangers I knew lurked in the darkness, these encounters reminded me that, in so many cases, people truly still look out for each other.

Around noon on Thursday, four days in, Edwin and the kids arrived to take over from Lionel. Dexter and Eliza's testing was done, and Edwin had pulled them out of school early with the teacher's blessing. We all met up on the side of the dusty desert road, and Edwin—knowing me as he does—immediately brought me some coffee. I sipped it gratefully, despite the heat, letting the caffeine wash away the roughest edges of my fatigue.

My family's presence, too, lifted me. Of course, Edwin always knows exactly what I need to hear, whether it's a tough-love push or a few motivating words. Each time he sent me off with fresh supplies and a hug, he'd snap photos, knowing we'd want a record of the journey later.

As for the kids, they see how much time and sweat I put into my training on a day-to-day basis, and I'm always grateful when they can experience firsthand the culmination of these efforts. They're playful and bring their own sense of adventure, and Edwin and I sometimes make different parenting decisions in how to handle their wild energy. (I had to quiet my mom-brain the time I looked back and saw them hanging out the windows of our SUV as he drove, for instance.) But I know they're absorbing the bigger picture too. I even saw Dexter messaging one of his buddies: "Yeah, my mom's finishing a 300-miler." He seemed proud and a little bit in awe. If you've ever met a teenage boy, you know what a huge feat it is to impress them enough that they express it in words!

Though I do give him a hard time about some of his moods, Dexter can be sweet and protective when it counts. As I neared Vegas, a man who'd been standing near a bus stop started following me while Edwin and the kids were still a ways back in the car. When they got close enough to see what was happening, Dexter hopped out and walked with me. The last mile, Eliza joined too.

By then, I'd switched back into my blade so I could run the final segment. I updated the other solo runners in the group chat, many of whom were already done and asking after me. The communal nature of the event floored me. Yes, there was a leaderboard and a winner—the amazing Parley Hannan, who finished in an incredible 85 hours and 53 minutes, about three and a half days—but truly, we were all out there to test our own limits and fuel our sense of adventure, and everyone supported each other along the way.

At no time was that clearer than when I approached the "Welcome to Vegas" sign, which was serving as our finish line. A tunnel of people was there waiting for me—so many of the other solo runners, Edwin of course, and my friends Tara and Tony, who'd driven out from Arizona to surprise me with a big handmade poster. "Jacky, you freaking did it!" it said. Under that, they'd written, in parentheses, "We knew you would."

"I did it! Yeah!" I yelled back, then finally reached the Vegas sign, having covered, thanks to all the detours, a total of 300 miles. I embraced the blue wooden pole of the sign and raised my other arm in the air in victory. Someone handed me a can of hard seltzer and then a bottle of champagne, a Speed Project tradition. Edwin wrapped his arms around me, and in his embrace, the enormity of what I'd just done washed over me. I sobbed messy tears of joy and relief and exhaustion, all the things I'd seen and felt and overcome ebbing through me. The journey didn't go exactly the way I'd planned it—but that was a huge part of the point, in the end. I'd made success happen on my own terms, through my own grit and will, and I'll never forget it.

I learned, later, that not everyone shared Tara and Tony's certainty I would prevail. After the event, Lionel, the film crew that was following me, and even some of my friends in North Carolina and Arizona told me that, especially after I bruised my stump and couldn't run much anymore, they wondered if I would call it quits.

But Edwin and the kids never doubted me, and I never doubted myself. When you're running 300 miles across the desert on a prosthetic, you never know exactly what's going to happen. But my entire life has been about adapting to challenges. I'll do what I have to do to keep moving, whatever the pace.

Your path might not involve aggressive dogs, naps in the bed of a pickup, or pavement so hot that a bit of melted tar sticks to your tread. Yet whatever your adventure or obstacle, I'm here to tell you that the fastest speed or the shortest route isn't always the best.

Slow down if that's what it takes. Remember that if you have to veer off the main path, detours can take you to beautiful destinations as well. Life is made up of the small victories that add up to bigger ones. Forward is a pace, and progress is progress, however you make it.

11

BUILD A TEAM

Marathon 92 of 104

Right on Hereford. Left on Boylston. As I made one of the running world's most well-known turns—the final 90-degree bend of the Boston Marathon—I could barely hear myself think. One voice, that of my dear North Carolina friend Rachel Zelibor, rose above the din of the cowbells and loudspeakers. "Go, Jacky, go!" she yelled. "You can't stop now. You're making that podium."

Marathon number 92 was the only official race of my whole record-breaking effort, and it was a huge one. For both elite and amateur runners, the Boston Marathon represents the pinnacle of performance. It's the world's oldest annual marathon, and it maintains strict qualifying standards for entry. It's held every third Monday in April, on Patriots' Day. For this regional holiday, many businesses close for the day, and crowds of locals use it to come cheer the runners on their journey from suburban Hopkinton back into the heart of the city.

I was fortunate enough to qualify during the 2016 Chicago Marathon, and I ran Boston for the first time in 2018. The weather that year was historically, epically terrible, with wind gusts up to 45 miles an hour, pouring rain, and temperatures only in the 40s. I tried my hardest to persevere, but I was pulled off the course after the 15-mile mark, stumbling and shaking. I was far from the only runner to DNF due to hypothermia that day, but the experience still haunted me.

So when race organizers reached out and asked me to return in 2022 to compete in the newly established Para Athletics Division, I was excited. Not only could I get a do-over on this iconic course, I could compete against others in my classification—single below-the-knee amputees using prosthetics—for prize money. It seemed like an incredible opportunity to show what we could do, and to raise more funds for Amputee Blade Runners while I was at it. Plus, that year's race marked the fiftieth anniversary of women first being allowed to compete—a milestone that resonated deeply with me as a female athlete.

But I didn't say yes immediately, knowing there were a lot of logistics to consider. Phoenix to Boston is a five-hour flight, and then there was the expo, the lengthy bus ride from Boston to the starting line in Hopkinton on race morning, and the fact that I'd have to run my own personal marathons in the days surrounding the race too. Especially given how fatigued I was from all the mileage, I needed someone to help me think through all this. And if I did choose to run, I knew I'd want a support runner to join me on the course, an opportunity extended to every competitor in my category.

I couldn't ask Edwin to come, because the kids once again had testing the week of the race, and they needed at least one of us at home. But if there was anyone else I could trust to help me think through the decision and its implications, it was Rachel. We share a passion for doing things that others wouldn't even consider; she would never shoot down an idea just because it seemed a little "out there." Plus, she's a super-planner who's nearly always training for an ultra herself, a detail that made it feasible for her to jump into a full 26.2-mile race—or really, a few, since I'd want her to join me for the runs on the other days of the trip—on relatively short notice. That was key, because it was only a week before the event when I shot her a text. "What do you think about Boston?" I wrote. "I might run it. If I do, would you go with me?"

She immediately called me. "Okay, Jacky, the cat's out of the bag," she said. It turns out, she'd been talking with Edwin about coming out to support me for my 100th marathon, which would be happening just about a week after Boston. "But if you'd rather have me in Boston instead, I'm there for you. First, though, let's see if it's even possible."

She spent the next day researching flights, for me and for her, and texting me the list of pros and cons. The travel would be draining, and if things went awry, I might have to get creative about getting in all my marathons to keep my record going. I had brief visions of running 26.2 miles around an airport! But the opportunity to redeem my past Boston experience while elevating parasport was compelling…

“I think you should do it,” she wrote, and I agreed. “Let’s make it happen.”

I left for Boston on Thursday night, and the race was Monday, which meant I had to run three marathons around the city before the big one, and then another before my flight home on Tuesday. It was somewhat ridiculous: What other Boston runner had a marathon for a shakeout run, and another as a recovery run? Fortunately, Rachel was the ultimate guide and wingwoman, charting routes through Boston’s Back Bay, Chinatown, and other neighborhoods.

By this point, my social media following had grown, and there were a few articles in the media about what I was attempting. Boston is always teeming with runners and fans of the sport throughout the weekend before Marathon Monday, but I wasn’t expecting so many people around town to recognize me and stop me. I found the attention a little embarrassing at first. But Rachel never failed to hype me up, always piping in to share more about my goals and accomplishments, and I tried my best to be a good sport. A few selfies in, I relaxed and embraced the encounters as part of my mission.

On race morning, the skies were mercifully clear, and the temperature was just about perfect: 54°F. Rachel and I rode the bus to the start with superstars of the marathon world (including 2018 Boston champion Des Linden), then waited in a private area of the Athletes’ Village until it was time to walk to the starting line.

The para-athletes started five minutes after the elite women. I stood there, looking across the road at all the blades and the tethers binding visually impaired runners to their guides, feeling the bundle of nerves and excitement each of us brought to the event. I was near tears as I contemplated the significance. Instead of being accused of cheating by running with a blade, I was competing in a category that honored my differences.

Then the gun sounded and we were off. With thirty thousand runners in total and an estimated half a million spectators, most points along the 26.2-mile route were packed and deafening. After so many quiet, solo miles, the juxtaposition was, at times, overwhelming. But Rachel served as a fabulous buffer, making sure there was enough space around me that no one tripped me or bumped my blade. She had patience for when I needed to slow down or walk for a minute—this happened a couple of times on the uphills—and in a reversal from the days before, she kindly turned down the people who asked me to stop and take a photo mid-race. "She's running right now," Rachel would say. "Catch us after the finish line!"

She also knew, though, when I needed a little push. As the course flattened out, she encouraged me to pick up the pace. There might have been moments when I wanted to punch her in the face, but deep down I was incredibly grateful.

With about six miles to go, Rachel spotted two familiar runners ahead. One was Adrianne Haslet, who survived the Boston Marathon bombings in 2013 and who also runs with a below-the-knee prosthetic. She was a huge driving force in getting the para division included for the first time in the previous year's race. Her support runner was none other than Shalane Flanagan, an Olympic silver medalist who'd won the New York City Marathon in 2017, the first American woman to do so since 1977.

My respect for these women was overwhelming. But when I was out on the course, they also represented my competition—racers who were looking for the best out of themselves, just like I was.

Rachel innately understood just how I felt, and knew how to harness it. "Jacky," she said. "I know you're tired, but it's go time. Adrianne is going to do her best to stay in front of you. If you pass her and hold on, you can make the podium."

By then, every muscle fiber was feeling the 92 marathons I'd run in the months prior. We were making the final climb up the infamous Heartbreak Hill, and I wanted so badly to walk, even just for a moment, for relief. But I knew Rachel was right, and I tuned in to the sounds of the crowd, letting their whoops and applause carry me forward. As we began to hit the downhill, we passed Adrianne and Shalane and didn't look back. In the end, I placed third by 13 minutes.

Performance wasn't my primary goal. Afterward, though, I couldn't help but be incredibly proud of both Adrianne and myself, as well as the first- and second-place finishers, Paralympians Liz Willis and Melissa Stockwell. We'd stepped up and brought parasport to the forefront, blazing a new trail for other athletes to follow, just like the first official women finishers had done back in 1972.

That night, Rachel and I—along with other luminaries, including Linden and Meb Keflezighi, who won the men's race in 2014—gathered for dinner at a nearby hotel, sharing stories of the course and picking up our awards. At one point, Rachel glanced over at me, her eyes wide. "This is surreal," she said. "I'm never doing another marathon unless I get VIP status again! Jacky, I'm so grateful you included me."

For a moment, I wasn't sure how to answer. "Rachel, what do you mean? You did so much for *me,* even when I was a grouch in the middle of the race," I said. "I'm the grateful one."

She tilted her glass toward me and smiled. "Well, let's just say I think we make a pretty good team," she replied.

~

Humans are hardwired for cooperation and connection, but asking for support can still feel awkward at best, and sometimes nearly impossible. Psychologists and other experts point to many reasons for this phenomenon. For some of us—raising my hand high here!—it stems back to a childhood in which we were made to feel shame and guilt for having physical or emotional needs.

As we get older, we might worry that asking for help makes us seem weak. In a culture that often prides itself on rugged individualism, we can get the idea that heroes are self-made and that we "should" be able to handle everything ourselves. We might look around and see others who seem to have it all together—or conversely, see people who have what seem like bigger problems, which leads us to question whether we even "deserve" a helping hand.

I know all those influences swirled around in my head early on after my cancer diagnosis and surgery. As I've noted, though, in the years since, I quickly learned to do everything I could do before my amputation, and some of it better than ever. I didn't want to feel pitied or different, and I became so well-practiced at hiding my prosthetic that many people didn't even know I had it. I couldn't fault people outside my innermost circle for not realizing I might need support, because I never let on that there was anything wrong. That said, the loneliness I felt undoubtedly contributed to the feelings of depression that followed.

The truth of the matter is that I really couldn't do everything on my own. No one can, regardless of their level of ability or disability. Trying to push your way through hardships alone makes life much harder than it has to be, and it also robs us of the incredible power of community and the gift of both giving and receiving support.

Running has reinforced this for me, time and again. Yes, it's an individual sport—it's your name on the registration form, you're the one who pins on a bib with your number and timing chip, and your legs carry you across the finish line. Yet there isn't a single accomplishment, whether it's an Olympic medal in the 100 meters or a 200-mile belt buckle, that belongs solely to one athlete. There's always a team behind everyone, from the best-known superstars in their sports to the amateur athletes. We all have some combination of coaches, medical professionals, dietitians, sport psychologists, training partners, and family and friends too.

Sometimes, the team aspect is more literal and apparent. In 2018, a friend told me about an application to run the Vermont City Marathon with Team MEB, led by none other than the Boston Marathon champion. He was interested in runners with inspiring stories or who had overcome obstacles to participate in the sport. I filled out an application, was interviewed for a slot, and was one of four people selected.

On race weekend, it was a true joy to meet with the other athletes he'd chosen. One was a college student who survived a car accident and committed herself to distance running afterward, serving as president of her university's running club. Another was a triathlete who'd nearly died and spent ten days in a coma after colliding with a car on his bike. The third was a twelve-year-old Somalian refugee who'd never run a race before but wanted to show her family—and the world—just what was possible.

And of course, there was Meb, who came to the United States as a child as a refugee from Eritrea and went on to win an Olympic silver medal, write bestselling books, and claim victory in Boston in 2014, uniting the running community and the whole country the year after the horrific bombings. Despite—or perhaps because of—all he's been through, he's one of the humblest and kindest people I've ever met. And he rarely forgets a face. To this day, if I see him at a race or other event, he says hello and asks about me, Edwin, and the kids.

Before the race, Meb met with us, signed copies of his book, and passed along his advice for running and for life. "The marathon isn't easy—it's a grind," he told us. "But remember, winning isn't about getting first place. It's about getting the best out of yourself."

As I looked around at my teammates, all with different stories but united in our common goal, I understood that we'd be pulling the best out of each other—and that I was a part of something bigger than one person or one race. As the former *Runner's World* editor and

another Boston Marathon champion, Amby Burfoot, once wrote: "Running is ultimately a personal experience. It is a revival of the spirit, a private oasis for the thirsty mind. Yet, its healing power only increases in the presence of others. Run together and the oasis grows cooler and more satisfying."

That day, we put on our matching "Meb's Team" shirts and ran our own section of the course, each of us taking over for another. Right before the finish line, we joined back together, holding hands to complete the race in just a little under three and a half hours. In that moment, the times I'd been treated as an outsider by the running community melted away. I'd never felt more connected to the sport, or so deeply aware of how much more memorable our victories can be when we share them.

~

When it comes to trail and ultrarunning, there's a huge component of collaboration even when you're not on a relay team. Once you get to distances of 50 miles and above, most runners recruit a crew and pacers to support them in their efforts. Pacers run with you during some portion of your miles, helping to set the tempo and keep your mindset positive. They're also on point for knowing the route, encouraging you to eat and drink, and giving the crew updates on your progress.

Crew members, meanwhile, are like the mobile versions of a pit crew at a car race—the behind-the-scenes heroes who travel around the course, usually by car, meeting you at aid stations to make sure you're all set with food, fluids, and supplies. Exactly what this looks like depends on the runner and the race. As I've mentioned before, some runners are highly organized, creating detailed spreadsheets down to the minute and the gram of carbohydrate. I'm a lot more relaxed and spontaneous, in large part because I can't always be sure exactly how any given mile or ultramarathon will go. Signing up to crew me means knowing you'll need to expect the unexpected and do lots of quick thinking and decision-making along the way.

Regardless of how detailed or vague the plans are, crewing is a huge responsibility that involves game-time calls and high-stress situations. Essentially, a runner who asks you to crew is putting much of their fate in your hands. Your job starts with managing logistics and getting them what they need, when they need it, whether that's a snack or an ice pack or, in my case, a spare leg! At every aid station, you must anticipate anything that might help them and then be able to either have it ready or fetch it quickly.

But it doesn't stop there. Another major component of crewing and pacing is essentially becoming an extension of your runner's brain, making decisions for them and keeping them motivated when they're dragging. At the beginning of the race, the runner will share their bigger goal, whether that's beating the cutoffs or achieving a certain finish time, and from then on, that becomes a shared ambition, one that may require the crew to show some tough love to help the runner achieve.

In the middle to late miles of a 100- or 250-mile effort, it's difficult for a runner to think straight, decide what to eat, or remember exactly why they signed up for this bonkers event in the first place. It's up to you, the crew, to remind them. They may sit down to change shoes and stay there; you'll strongly encourage them to get up. They might claim they're not hungry, but you know they need to get their calories in, so you hand them a potato or demand they sip on a cup of broth or a Coke. When they start to document all the ways the race is going poorly, you counter them with signs of success. If they insist they really don't care anymore, they're so tired, and they just want to quit, well, you just have to tell them you know they're fatigued, but they *do* care, and that, deep down, they really want to keep going.

Of course, you can't force them. In cases where their physical or mental well-being is in danger, it's also your role to help them make the right call to quit. Most of the time, though, the battles runners face in the tough miles are mental ones that can be conquered. They often just need someone to remind them they're capable of doing so.

~

In my mind, there's something so fundamental and fulfilling about the experience of crewing and pacing, or being crewed or paced. First, if you're the runner, you have to reach out and ask someone to join your support team in the first place—not always the easiest thing to do. Then, you must be very clear on your goals and able to share them clearly and in a way that allows your people to step up and help you achieve them.

Each meeting point or aid station (or each mile, if you're being paced) becomes a back-and-forth, where one person expresses their needs, and one or more others fulfills those needs. It's quite beautiful, really, even if there are sometimes curse words and extra bodily fluids!

If your crew has more than one person, it makes sense to divide the tasks according to each person's skills and expertise. The member with the best navigation skills handles the driving and parking (heads-up—that's never going to be me!), while the timely one keeps an eye on the clock, the most organized one lays out all the supplies in advance of the runner's arrival, and the least squeamish one can take on the role of foot care. It's not unusual for ultrarunners to need someone to add more lube, to patch hot spots with tape, or even to pop blisters. But everyone stands by, ready to troubleshoot unexpected issues, change strategies based on how a race unfolds, and otherwise jump in where needed to get their runner to the finish line.

It's a lot of work on behalf of someone else, and yet when you're crewing or pacing, you also must take care of your own health and well-being. It's a long day (and sometimes night) out there for the whole team, not just the runner. You have to think ahead about getting your own fuel, planning your bathroom breaks, and getting rest when you need it. It's like what they say about putting the oxygen mask on yourself before helping others who need assistance: If you can't breathe or think straight, you're not going to be any good at tending to others.

Aside from the camaraderie, you also often come away from crewing having learned something. You may, for instance, walk away with ideas and strategies to improve your own racing. Several years ago, I supported Callie Vinson, who completed an FKT—or fastest known time—on the 250-mile Maricopa Trail, close to where I live in Arizona. Because an FKT isn't an organized event, there are no aid stations whatsoever, and a runner and their crew must supply everything needed to sustain the effort, from fuel to water to toilet tissue.

I was one of more than two dozen people who stepped up to lend a hand over the 103 hours she was running. To make our jobs as easy as possible, Callie had detailed notes about who was on point for what and when. She kept all her supplies in neatly organized plastic tubs, which made it easy for her crew to know which to haul out at each stop.

My role was to pace Callie for about 22 miles, starting at 11:00 p.m. on her final night. By then, she'd run close to 200 miles already and was very tired. I stayed next to her, stride for stride, doing everything I could to keep her awake—talking, singing, telling stories, cracking jokes. At times, she'd fall silent. I could tell she needed me to be quiet too, so she could process the discomfort and fatigue she was going through. Like crewing, pacing can make or break a runner, and I had to use my instincts and experience to read her state of mind and keep her moving forward.

Her boyfriend, Scott, was tracking us. At one point, he met us with her car and her labeled bins so she could replenish her fluid and fuel stores. Seven hours after we started, as the sun began to rise, I delivered her to the friend who was waiting to pace her for the final miles. I'll never be able to plan to her level of detail, but the experience made me realize that sketching out a few basics in advance can make life easier on my crew and pacers. Now, I do my best to share the potential outcomes with them beforehand, going over the tools I carry with me and what I'll need in the event that I decide to change legs.

Indeed, crewing and being crewed have taught me that clear communication is crucial. Everyone needs to know if a runner is going to be 5 minutes early or 10 minutes behind, and to be clear on who's refilling the water bottles versus who's snapping photos. Even if you do have a plan and a chain of command, minor squabbles will likely still pop up, including with your fatigued, sleep-deprived runner. As you gain experience, you learn not to take things personally. Any hard feelings typically tend to fade in the frenzy of celebrating your runner's finish or in the post-race beverages you'll enjoy together, regardless of whether the goal was achieved.

All this may sound a bit overwhelming and complicated, but it's a magnificent type of chaos—and honestly, it's also a whole heck of a lot of fun. Something magical happens when you spend an entire day (or more) in the great outdoors with a group of other people who share a common mission. You bond by working as a team, solving problems together, and, in the end, you realize you're all bigger than your differences.

~

When you're the runner out on the course, knowing your crew has your back is a powerful performance enhancer. Even if you run without a pacer, anticipating a smiling face—and a helping hand—when you reach the next aid station can truly make the difference between pushing ahead and falling apart.

Research actually bears out this phenomenon. Sometimes, even more than the support you receive, it's your sense of *perceived* support that gives you the resilience you need to keep going. If you expect your crew to be there for you when things go awry, you feel that much stronger and more capable, both before you encounter a challenge and when an unexpected obstacle arises.

I know I felt this in 2023 during the Yeti 100-miler, a run along the scenic Virginia Creeper Trail in Virginia. Jeannette was crewing me, and I was feeling great—going faster than I'd planned through the earlier miles. Each time we connected at the first four aid stations, she greeted me with an enthusiastic, "How are you feeling?" We talked about what I'd eaten—Nutella peanut butter wraps and bacon, among other goodies—as she took photos and video for posterity and social media.

It was already dark when we parted after the 56-mile mark, at the aid station at Taylor Valley. I knew I'd be on my own for the next 7-plus miles. It wasn't long after I took off that my headlamp died. Much of this course is near water, and now I couldn't see if I was going to topple into it. I tried to shine the flashlight on my Garmin watch onto the trail ahead of me and listen for the sounds of the rushing stream. But then I heard something else emerge from the darkness—a loud voice, one that sounded threatening.

I nearly held my breath as I attempted to gauge what the voice was saying and where it was coming from. The words didn't make any sense, but the tone was clearly angry. Was it getting closer? Farther away? I couldn't determine. I slowed to a walk, hoping desperately that my steps didn't allow the owner of the voice to find me before I located him. I pulled out my phone—just in case—and found I had no signal, no way of communicating with anyone. Now, I went from unsure to terrified. "Jacky, stay calm," I thought to myself. "You know Jeannette is just ahead. You can get to her."

I kept going, slowly and cautiously. After what felt like an eternity, I finally saw a light ahead of me, and then realized it was attached to a person—another runner! A sense of relief washed over me; I was still on the right trail, and there were other athletes nearby. My spirits lifted even more when I realized the runner was standing still, waiting for me. Word had spread that a loose cannon of a man had camped out in the forest and was unhappy that the race was encroaching on his territory, so runners began pairing up for safety. With my new friend's company—not to mention the glow of his headlamp—I did my best to pick up the pace again.

Jeannette, meanwhile, was freaking out. She'd been counting

down the hours, expecting me to arrive back at the aid station far earlier. The other crew members and race volunteers were also discussing the threatening presence, and Jeannette, who couldn't contact me or see my location, feared the worst. Eventually, she started running backward along the course, toward me. It didn't take long for us to connect, and when we did, she opened her arms and I collapsed into her.

"Jacky, oh my gosh, you're okay. I'm so sorry I wasn't with you. I was so scared. I'm so glad you're here," she cried.

"I was so scared too," I answered. "But you *were* with me. I could feel it. I knew I had to get back here to you." Our tears spoke volumes—of fear and distress, yes, but also gratitude and love. I hope you never have to experience something like that during a race, but if you do, I hope you have your own Jeannette there to embrace you on the other side.

~

To receive that type of support, you have to recruit a crew in the first place, and as I mentioned, that first step is often the hardest. But just like it's worth pushing through the tough spots in races, this is one of those difficulties that demands persistence and perseverance. Remind yourself that you're worthy of support. Get clear on what you need, whether that's someone to pace you step for step or to meet you somewhere along the way. Then, set aside your ego and your fears of rejection, and ask for it. Not everyone will be able to show up every single time, or to play every role, and that's okay. The bigger your potential pool of crew members, the easier the tasks ahead of you will feel.

I've learned this lesson again and again—after cancer, during my bouts of postpartum depression, and when I've hit a snag or a setback with my running. I know I'll always be stubborn, with an independent streak, but when I finally admit that I need help, and ask for it—whether that's being more vulnerable with Edwin, speaking to my doctor honestly about my mental health, or calling a friend to crew me—I can feel a burden lifted. And when I can offer someone else support in return, I have a deep sense of fulfillment, as if I'm honoring my larger purpose.

In a way, life is just one big relay race, where sometimes we're the runner and sometimes we're the crew. When I have a moment of hesitation about asking for help, I remember just how meaningful it is to be a part of someone else's team. Sharing our joys magnifies them, as I learned when I whooped in celebration as Callie nabbed her FKT at Maricopa. Navigating challenges together makes each barrier feel that much more surmountable, something I realize each time Edwin, Jeannette, or Rachel troubleshoots a mid-race problem with me. And even holding our losses together makes our grief more bearable.

I say it all the time: You never really know what someone else is going through. When I first met my friends Mike and Alisa—initially through Instagram, and then in real life, since they live a street away—I thought they were some of the nicest people I'd come across in a while. Alisa is an oncology nurse, so we bonded immediately when talking about cancer. Soon, I'd learn they'd experienced immense tragedy, having lost one son to a drug overdose and another to a motorcycle accident, all within a year. Still, they never failed to show up for others, including joining me when I asked for group support during my marathon record runs.

When I was in the midst of Project "I Can Do Hard Things" the year prior—during which I ran a half marathon each day for 250 days, to honor my twenty-first anniversary of being cancer-free—I dedicated one of my runs to their sons. They joined me, and we talked about their boys, two lives cut short before their time. Mike and Alisa have since dedicated a bench on the San Tan Mountain Trail in their sons' memories, and when we run together and come to it, we stop. That brief pause, that moment of reflection, assures them that their family's story transcends their losses, and that we'll carry their sons' legacy with us as we run forward, together.

12

DON'T FORGET THE DUCT TAPE!

Marathon 100 of 104

Day 100. My original goal. By now, though, I knew I needed to keep going. A couple of weeks earlier, I'd found out that another runner was chasing the record and had hit 101 consecutive marathons—so 102 became my new target.

Not long before mile 10, I felt a familiar sensation. My blade started slipping, ever so slightly, underneath me. I knew what that meant. The tread Edwin and I had affixed to the bottom of my blade was coming loose.

I kept going as far as I could, around the loop at Veterans Oasis, cursing myself for not putting the duct tape in my Jeep. I almost always keep some close by for days just like this one. Today—more than 2,500 miles into the challenge—I was just so tired I forgot.

Within a few steps, the tread had peeled almost completely off, nearly causing me to trip. "Hold up," I said to my friends Jenn and Mike, who'd joined me for the shuffle that day. "I'm going to have to fix this before I continue."

Without the tape, I had to call for backup: Edwin.

"Honey, I have a problem," I said. "It's the tread. It's come apart again." Fortunately, he was between meetings, so he drove the ten minutes over to the park with a bottle of super glue. I had to wait for him to get there—and then wait at least another ten minutes for the glue to dry. Fortunately, I had remembered to pack my walking foot! So I switched to that for a loop, and the three of us continued forward.

~

From the time I started running, I expected the sport to challenge my heart, legs, and lungs. Quickly, I understood how much mental strength was involved too. But especially as I got deeper into the trail and ultra world, I realized I'd also need hefty doses of creativity, problem-solving, and engineering skills. When you're always stretching the outer bounds of what your body and your equipment can handle, you'll need to be more than a little resourceful as things start to go sideways.

When I first took my original running blade, the Catapult, onto the trails, I noticed a few limitations. One of the first was how quickly I would wear through the tread on the bottom of the blade. I swear, it would only last about 5 miles before it disintegrated! That's a big nuisance when you're training for triple-digit mileage. Also, that blade was made for smooth roads, not trails, and I was always worrying I'd slip while crossing a stream or flying downhill.

One day, I had a thought. Could I cut the sole off the bottom of a shoe and repurpose it as a blade tread? After all, I wasn't using any of my left running shoes. (While I do wear a shoe with my walking foot, they don't go on a running blade.) With Edwin's help, I stripped the remaining tread off my blade, dissected a road running shoe, and fused the two together with super glue.

Our method wasn't perfect, and the tread wasn't nearly as grippy as a trail shoe's would be, but it was an improvement. And that experiment further showed me that I didn't have to just accept what was offered. I could take the situation into my own hands and, challenge by challenge, build a tool kit to overcome them.

The duct tape was a later addition. One of the first times I took this new tread for a spin was during the TransRockies race in August 2019. On day 1—after I got terrible blisters, but before I tumbled to the ground—I noticed that dirt had lodged underneath the tread, loosening it. Worried about falling, I'd borrowed some bandages from a fellow racer and used them to stick the tread back on around the edges. When I reached the aid station, volunteers replaced the bandages with some duct tape. While I finished that day's miles, the race director went out and bought me some super glue, which I used to reaffix the tread that evening.

We all face challenges en route to our big goals. Some solutions are big—a surgery, a new running blade, a dramatic life change. But others are as simple as a sticky piece of adhesive and a little creativity. Often, that's all you need to keep moving forward.

~

When I got the Fillauer Obsidian blade, the tread made a major improvement in my running. It was tire-grade, with deeper grooves specifically designed to adhere better to a wide range of surfaces. I put it to the test in the gnarliest conditions and found it a significant improvement over both the original Catapult tread and our home-baked shoe-dissection experiment. Now when I stepped on a wet rock, I no longer went sliding, and when I headed down a steep incline, I could put my weight firmly into my blade, without fear of accidentally sliding on my rear.

Even so, the tread didn't last forever. As my mileage totals increased and the surfaces I was covering grew more treacherous, I was lucky if I could get six months out of each piece of tread before it came loose or wore down so much it lost its grip. This meant that, at least twice a year, I had to head back to the prosthetist's office for a tune-up.

That was my routine until late 2019, when I had to make another change. I had the Algonquin 50K coming up in February, and my tread was worn out. My prosthetist, Chandler, was on vacation, which meant there'd be an even longer delay than usual to get the tread replaced.

I was tired of having to wait for an appointment before I could get back to training the way I wanted to. So once again, Edwin and I took things into our own hands. We called the prosthetist's office and asked if they could order the tread and have us pick it up. Then, Edwin and I took our own set of tools to the task, removing the remnants of the old tread and gluing on a new one.

The result? No shade on Chandler, but I couldn't tell the difference between a tread he'd applied and our version. "Nice," I teased Edwin. "You've now earned yourself yet another job: tread replacement technician."

His grin let me know he wasn't upset about the new title. "Hey, at least I'm good for something around here besides brewing coffee!" he joked back.

Now we always have a stash of several new replacement treads, which we've picked up in advance. At this point, Edwin has the process down pat. He sits at the kitchen table with the necessary implements: a flathead screwdriver, a couple of knives, sandpaper, super glue, the new tread, and a beer or a coffee, depending on the time of day.

First, he pries up the remainder of the old tread using the screwdriver, then finishes separating it with a good old kitchen steak knife. (Don't worry, we have a separate one specifically for this purpose.) He uses a utility knife to scrape off the remnants of the old glue before lightly sanding the blade's surface—just enough to ensure it's glue-free, and taking care not to damage the carbon fiber.

Then, he preps the new tread by applying an ample amount of super glue. (The brand he uses is Loctite Super Glue Gel Control; it's thick enough not to run, and the bottle design makes it easier to apply than with a messy metal tube.) He squeezes the glue both on the inside of the tread and on the outside of my blade, including a dab on the top where the end of the tread wraps over for a more secure fit. Then, he brings the two pieces together, pressing them firmly to bond them.

Once the new tread is affixed to the blade, I try to wait a full twenty-four hours before running on it, so the glue sets. Sometimes, though, I lose my patience. I've been known to put zip ties around the tread, for an extra layer of insurance, and then head out the door earlier. With that little bit of extra confidence in place before the glue is 100 percent dry, I haven't had an issue.

None of this is to suggest that experts don't matter or that you have to take every problem, small or large, on your own shoulders. But just as I've learned to advocate for myself in a wide range of medical situations, I've also realized you don't always need to get the higher-ups involved when there's an issue you can address yourself. Regaining control of this part of the process meant I didn't have to wait for anyone else when my tread was trashed. I felt powerful and competent, and I knew that, especially with Edwin in my corner, I now had far more agency over my athletic endeavors.

~

Another thing I've had to figure out for myself is sweat management. Every runner sweats. What you might not have considered, especially if you haven't run with a blade, is exactly where your sweat goes. For most runners, it evaporates into the air or splashes down onto the trail or pavement. When your stump is covered up by a silicone liner and a socket, however, your perspiration can't escape. Add to that the fact that your stump may sweat more than your leg used to because of changes to your nervous system after trauma and surgery. The result? Your stump winds up soaked. Not only does this lead to painful chafing and irritation, it can even cause your blade to slide right off. So the problem is far more than a minor irritation; this is actually the number one issue I get asked about by other amputees when they're first getting started in the sport.

When I began running, I used a vacuum system to attach my socket to my running foot. I wore an outer sleeve that went over both my socket and my leg, forming a seal that kept my leg in my socket. This meant my stump got very, very slick! I found I had to take my leg off every five miles or so to dump out the perspiration. Needless to say, that wasn't going to work as I continued to ramp up in distance, especially given that I was running first in North Carolina and then in Arizona. Yes, in Arizona it's a dry heat, but 100°F is still going to make you a hot mess!

Every amputee has different preferences; some people swear by the vacuum. But for me, switching to a suction system—where the liner and socket fit closely together, and air is pushed out through a valve at the bottom—improved the situation considerably. Still, I needed to figure out a way to handle the remainder of the moisture.

My prosthetist suggested applying heavy-duty deodorant to my stump at night. You essentially rub it all over, and when it dries, you towel it off. When I tried this, I did perspire less, but my skin became red and irritated from the chemicals. The reaction should not have been surprising, since I have a skin condition called vitiligo, which decreases the pigment in my skin and makes it more sensitive. However, it did mean that—frustratingly—I had to keep searching for a solution.

Some people take medications that can reduce sweating,

and some even get Botox injections, which block the action of a neurotransmitter called acetylcholine that stimulates sweat glands. I'm glad there are options, but I was nervous about risks and side effects. And in the case of Botox, which lasts only a few months, I didn't want to have to get repeated shots.

For me, the best solution wound up being relatively simple: a sweat-wicking sock. Even then, I had to try a few different brands to find one that worked. The first one I tried was so thick it tore up my skin almost as much as running in my old walking foot—but again, I know that one works great for some people. It's so individual! I Googled around for other options before hitting the jackpot: the Knit-Rite Liner-Liner Prosthetic Sock with X-Static.

This sock is super thin and stretchy, so it fits snugly between my stump and my liner, and it feels soft and comfortable against my skin. Just like a running sock for your foot, it wicks away moisture and fights bacteria that cause odors and irritation. The downside is that it's a bit pricey—usually $20 for a single sock—and has to be replaced frequently. I look at it as an investment in keeping my skin healthy, no needles required.

~

Sometimes, the solutions that make the most sense are the ones that are less tangible and a lot more, well, human. I know I've mentioned that I don't have the best sense of direction, and trail races can be especially hard to navigate because I often have my head down to watch for roots and rocks rather than looking up to see the trail markers. So perhaps it's not a shocker that, more than once, I've taken a wrong turn and gotten lost in a race.

About 10 miles into the Uwharrie 20-miler in 2019, I found myself in a pickle. It was only my second trail race, and I was undoubtedly in over my head. As the trail wound its way through the Uwharrie National Forest in North Carolina, I'd already had to bum-shuffle my way across a log to complete a water crossing. (This race, by the way, was the one that convinced me I absolutely had to get trekking poles.) The race directions flat-out say that you should expect to trip and fall at least once, that even experienced trail runners are prone to lose their way, and that if you do, you're liable to enter a hunting area. Yikes!

Of course, it wasn't long before I looked up and noticed there were no more white trail markers on the trees around me. I panicked but kept going…for the moment. Soon, I found myself in a huge open field. "This doesn't feel right at all," I thought. Fear coursed through me; my eyes filled with tears. I didn't know if I should go forward or backward. All I could think about, to be honest, was bears. Were there some nearby? And were they hungry?

I knew Edwin was waiting for me near the finish line, but I no longer had any idea where that was. So I called him, sobbing. "I—I'm in a field and I know I'm off course, but I don't know where or how, and I'm going to get eaten by a bear!" I managed to sputter.

"It's okay, Jacky, it's okay," he reassured me. "I'm going to come and find you. Stay right there. And if you see a bear, stay calm and move away slowly and sideways."

I can't say that his advice made me any less terrified—it was practical, but it didn't help reduce the mental pictures I formed of becoming some bear's lunch—but I did what he said. I shared my location on my phone so he could pinpoint where I was, and then I waited. After what seemed like an eternity but was probably just twenty minutes, he appeared on the other side of the field.

I was so grateful, I collapsed into his arms in a sweaty hug. "I'm so glad you're here—and I didn't get eaten by a bear!" I exclaimed.

"It's all right, Jacky," he said. "We'll run it in together." From there, I only had to follow him to make it to the finish line.

I have never gotten any better at directions, and that was far from the only time Edwin or the kids have had to come and "angel" me in from a spot that was a little (or a lot) off the prescribed course. I always do my best to follow markers, and I've also started uploading the course to my Garmin watch ahead of time, as I had for the Speed Project. And Edwin prepares too, carrying a course map with him and always wearing his running shoes, just in case.

As I already pointed out, asking for support as an independent woman and athlete is a whole other challenge. Yet as Edwin and I have worked together to solve running-related challenges, our partnership has only grown stronger and healthier. Repeatedly, he reminds me that I can do incredible things, and that I don't have to do them alone.

~

Training is a constant process of putting your heart and your muscles through a series of stressors—controlled ones, but situations that test your comfort zone nonetheless. As you recover from each session, you grow stronger and fitter, preparing yourself to take on even bigger challenges.

A similar sort of process occurs when it comes to your craftiness, resilience, and creativity—the tool kit you carry with you, literally and figuratively, to address unexpected turns in the road or new barriers that arise.

That, to me, is the other thrilling part of the extreme races I do. Not only do I learn that my body is more capable than I thought, I realize I can think my way out of tough spots too. Each time I come up with a solution to an unforeseen issue, I feel a thrill of accomplishment that helps carry me through to the finish line.

Duct tape, super glue, an extra sock. My tread, the wrench that adjusts my blade, and my trekking poles. The more races I've run and obstacles I've encountered, the bigger the tool kit I carry for managing them. I've long ago given up on the idea that things will go perfectly smoothly, since when I'm running with a blade, they never do. Instead, I recognize that my equipment—and my navigation—will sometimes fail, so I carry the things I need to fix the problem and carry on.

I know, though, that, unlike Edwin and Jeannette, I'm not the most organized athlete. Every once in a while, despite my past experiences, I leave something important behind. But that, too, creates an opportunity to change my mindset.

Yes, there are moments I curse myself and my perimenopausal brain fog when I forget something. I get upset when I have yet another barrier to cope with as an amputee. But I try to end the pity party quickly and channel my frustration into discovery. Once, I forgot the liner that goes with my blade as I headed to the Run at the Rock in Greensboro, North Carolina, a race Edwin and I were scheduled to run together. I was bummed at first that I wouldn't be able to participate, but then I took it as an opportunity to cheer him on and spectate the other runners, appreciating the entirely different view of the course.

Other times, when I forget the super glue or duct tape, I know that bandages and shoelaces can work in a pinch. They're not the most high-tech, glamorous, or long-term fixes, of course. Still, there are plenty of times when patching things together is a perfectly fine solution until you can properly address the underlying issue. Perfection isn't the goal when you're in the middle of a 100-miler or your 100th marathon. It's all about doing what you can to get through and keep running.

Your challenges may not be the same as mine. My guess, though, is that if you think back through your own complications and stumbling blocks, you'll realize all the ingenious ways you've come up with to navigate your version of loose treads. Some of those tools may be profound mental shifts—say, the skill of allowing yourself to grieve, of asking for help, or of reframing a challenge as an opportunity. Others are as small as carrying an extra sock, a few bandages, or, yes, a roll of duct tape.

The next time you're feeling lost or scared, make a conscious effort to open your tool kit and make an inventory of what's inside. You might even want to write down, or at least think through, the talents you've developed and the creative tools you've used to make things work when it counts. My guess is that you'll surprise yourself with all the grit, capability, and adaptiveness you've shown through the years.

We don't often pause to give ourselves credit for building up this repertoire of resilience, but we should. Remembering how we've solved one problem before can offer valuable insight on how to crack the next code. It also affords us the confidence we need to keep pushing when it's tough. You can do hard things, after all. Don't you ever forget it.

Believe me, there are plenty of times when I wish running were easier for me—when I wish I didn't have quite so many challenges to overcome in a sport that's already among the hardest out there. We all have moments when, in the depths of our struggle, we question why we've been dealt the hand we have, wishing for a life that's a bit smoother or more carefree.

But then, on those days when I have to pull out the duct tape, I take a moment to appreciate its silver sheen. In a way, it reminds me of the ancient Japanese art of kintsugi. When pottery is broken, it's often glued back together not with transparent glue but with lacquer mixed with powdered gold, silver, or platinum that shows where the break happened. Rather than trying to hide the damage, it's highlighted. The idea is that every break, every struggle, is part of the history of the object.

My prosthetic and the tools I use to maintain it are visible signs of my life story. It's been years since I last felt the urge to cover up my prosthetic or hide my disability; now, I don't even see them as imperfections. And even when my tread is stuck on with duct tape, I don't worry that people will think I'm falling apart.

For me, tools like super glue and duct tape are about much more than attaching some rubber bumps to the bottom of my foot. They represent how I've learned to solve problems as they arise. These tangible symbols of resourcefulness and hope show that I can keep things together, even when it feels like they're crumbling around me.

13

SET BIG GOALS, THEN ADAPT TO ACHIEVE

Marathon 103 of 104

If there was anything remarkable about marathon 103, it was just how unremarkable it was.

When I woke up on April 29, I was still feeling the buzz from the day prior, when I'd finished marathon 102 and officially broken the record. I thought of the crew of friends who came out to support me, cheering me on as I crossed our makeshift finish line. I smiled as I glanced over at the trophy Edwin had handed me, a blue glass figure holding a star. The base bore my name and my pending title: Guinness World Record Holder. He'd had to do a little editing of the next line, which originally read, "100 Marathons in 100 Consecutive Days." When the target had changed a few weeks prior, he'd taped the digit 2 over the end of each number to reflect my updated accomplishment. "We'll need to change that again," I thought to myself.

Though I'd now completed my original mission and then some, I wasn't done yet. A local brewery, Four Silos, had reached out earlier in the week. Yes, 102 is great, they said—but wouldn't 104 be better? If I extended my streak to include the number 4, they'd make me a shirt and throw me a celebration on Saturday, April 30, the day I'd finish. I thought about it and realized that it might be nice to have a little extra padding on the record, making it that much harder for the next person to break. Besides, a Saturday finish meant friends who had to work during the week would be able to come out and join the celebration.

"That sounds great," I wrote back. "Let's do it."

But between the hype of the 102 and the finality of 104, it was just me and 26.2 miles, solo. As I quietly made my laps around Veterans Oasis Park, it felt surreal that I'd not only made it to my original goal of 100, but I hadn't crumbled when the goalposts shifted. Back when I started, I truly wasn't sure if I could surpass 10 marathons in a row. Now here I was, going even longer than I'd planned.

That evening, as I ate and recovered, I received a surprising email with another offer. An agency working with RXBAR, makers of delicious and nutritious protein bars, told me the brand wanted to match any donations made to my fundraiser for Amputee Blade Runners by May 1. They'd go up to $104,000, to match the 104 marathons.

I was stunned. My original target was to raise enough for one or two blades, a total cost of between $10,000 and $20,000. Now, I had the opportunity to help more amputees than I could ever have dreamed. My total at that point was $23,358, already exceeding my original goal. However, now that I knew every dollar could go double the distance, I was even more motivated than ever to keep pushing.

Given the tight timeline, I rushed into action to get the word out. I posted on social media and alerted the traditional media outlets that had covered my efforts. Amputee Blade Runners pushed the message out to their network too.

None of this would have happened if I hadn't set a huge, ambitious goal of 100 marathons in the first place. Yet it also wouldn't have occurred if I'd stuck to my original intention instead of modifying my ambitions to fit the new circumstances. Things don't always work out the way you plan them, for better or worse. But if you can learn to go with the flow instead of fighting the current, you just might end up somewhere even better than you expected.

~

In my early days of running, success was narrowly defined. If I signed up for a 5K or a half marathon, I was bound and determined to finish it, and faster than I ever had. Like many new runners, I saw improvement quickly and almost became addicted to it.

As I gained experience and left the predictability of the roads for the unknown challenges of the trail, my perspective began to shift. Taking my blade to places it had never been meant I was opening the door to unexpected outcomes. Sometimes, things went worse than I hoped, or even worse than I feared. Often, though, an obstacle would lead to a new opportunity. I just had to work on accepting my new reality and finding the best path forward.

One such shift occurred due to circumstances far beyond my control. After finishing my first 50-miler at the Umstead ultra in April of 2019, I knew I wanted to go longer. So when I applied to run the 100-mile distance at the same race the following year and got an entry, I was thrilled. Between my training and racing on those trails, I knew them intimately, making this the perfect place to go for my first triple-digit distance. I officially started my training in November, with Edwin coaching me along the way.

Anyone alive in 2020 will be familiar with what happened next, between the fall of 2019 and the spring of 2020. As COVID-19 began to spread, races were canceled, one by one. First, the Boston Marathon—where I'd planned to return and try again in April, two years after my DNF—was postponed until the fall. Eventually, it'd be called off altogether, not to return until the following fall. Shortly afterward, I heard Umstead wouldn't be held either.

Of course, I understood why race organizers were making these choices. Everyone was doing their best to protect people from a disease that, at the time, was poorly understood. Still, I was disappointed. I'd been dreaming of that finish line since I'd crossed it at the 50-mile distance the year prior, and I'd logged hundreds of miles preparing for it. As it became apparent that life would be different for more than just a few weeks, I realized I'd need to be creative and make my own opportunities.

The first thing I tried was the 4x4x48 challenge, for which I ran

4 miles every 4 hours for 48 hours. At that time, running too far on the roads or trails was challenging because of COVID restrictions. No one yet knew for sure how the new virus spread, so some trails were closed altogether, and runners were under strict guidance about social distancing everywhere else they might train. I ended up doing most of my daytime miles on the treadmill at home and the rest up and down my street. That was no problem at, say, 1:00 a.m. and 5:00 a.m., when everyone else was asleep! I even snuck in a few extra miles, so by the end of the challenge, I'd logged 52 miles in total.

Although the mileage was relatively low, it wasn't an easy challenge. My stump didn't like all the stopping and starting, and I wound up swollen and bruised. The lack of sleep didn't feel great, either. Still, the feat reignited my joy of competing and testing my limits. What more could I do within the boundaries of these unusual circumstances, I wondered?

~

Scrolling on social media in the spring of 2020, I saw a post about the Aravaipa Strong Virtual Race. There were plenty of virtual 5Ks and even marathons at the time, but I hadn't seen any virtual ultramarathons until I came across this one. You could choose from several distances, all the way up to 100 miles. All you had to do was run the mileage, record it on your GPS watch, and upload your results to their online dashboard afterward, and you'd get credit for the effort—including, if you ran the 100, a belt buckle.

I never imagined I could be intrigued by a virtual race, but in these circumstances, the prospect was compelling. With in-person events on hiatus for the foreseeable future, I was drawn to the idea of joining with others, even from afar. One hundred miles had been on my radar for a while now, and having external validation for my efforts, by way of official race results and a buckle, sounded good too. I signed up.

At first, I planned to run 100 miles around my neighborhood, completing the same half-mile loop two hundred times. Again, this was a time when people were so fearful of runners breathing on them, they'd cross the street just to get away. I didn't want to cause anyone else stress, nor did I want to wear a mask to run in 80°F heat. More than anything, I wanted to do my part to help everyone get back to normal.

The other option was the treadmill. That posed its own challenges; the machine we had was not an expensive one. We'd bought it years before, on sale, not truly realizing the demands I'd eventually put on it. Edwin despises the treadmill, so it was primarily mine, but the most I'd logged on it at one time was 10 miles, and going ten times that distance sounded daunting for me and the treadmill both.

Two factors eventually swayed me toward the moving belt. The first was that the age of the treadmill wound up being a good thing. Many of the newer models automatically switch off after three hours, but when I contacted NordicTrack, they informed me that this older version had no such feature. I could run for hours and hours without stopping if I wanted to.

But the even more compelling reason for using the machine was that, upon doing a little research, I saw that there was no documentation of an amputee running 100 miles on a treadmill. There it was again—that tingly sense of both anxiety and excitement, the call to action and adventure that lit a spark inside me. I could be the first!

"Edwin, I think I know how we can make this 100-miler even more special," I said.

He smiled as I explained my plan. "Jacky, it's brilliant," he said.

~

The night before a race, many runners take a photo of what's called a "flat runner"—an image of their outfit (or "kit," as athletes often call it), their shoes, and anything else they'll need to make the day a success. I laid out everything on the belt of my treadmill—my blade, my shorts and shirt, my watch, and my trusty Squirrel's Nut Butter anti-chafing cream—and posted it to my Instagram stories. Edwin even printed me out a bib with the number 1, so I included that too. I informed my followers that I was starting at eight the next morning. "Aiming to finish within 24 hours," I wrote. "This will be my longest treadmill run ever, and I will be the first amputee to ever do this." I followed that with a scream emoji for good measure. Remember, this was my first time hitting triple digits—I knew it wasn't going to be easy.

Edwin, meanwhile, adapted the role of crew for the pandemic era, doing everything he could to take care of my needs and also to involve others in my quest, albeit virtually. On a cardboard box in the spare bedroom that served as our home gym, he made a sign that said, "Aid station 1–20," and stocked it with snacks such as bananas, Spring Energy gels, pretzels, and peanut M&M's. On a whiteboard leaning against the wall, he wrote out four columns of numbers, from 1 to 100. "I'll cross each one off as you reach it," he said. "That way, everyone who's following along will know where you're at in the challenge."

I woke up early that morning, giving myself time for a full breakfast, my go-to oats and banana, so I'd start the day with plenty of fuel and energy. Then, I went about the things I'd usually do before a race: getting dressed, braiding my hair into two long pigtails, and making sure my GPS watch, which we'd calibrated to the treadmill, was fully charged. It was a surreal feeling to be getting ready for something huge, but not even leaving the house. Soon, it was just about time.

I handed my social media channels over to Edwin, and moments before 8:00 a.m., he took us live on Instagram. I introduced myself and him and invited viewers to follow along with my efforts.

"Why are you doing this, Jacky?" Edwin asked me on camera, knowing there were likely people tuning in who couldn't conceive of spending an entire day running to nowhere.

"Well, all my 100-milers have been canceled," I said. "I'm doing it for myself, mostly. But it's exciting, because I'll be the first amputee to ever do this. I like pushing boundaries with the prosthetic and showing what's possible. If you've got the will, you can achieve anything you want."

And with that, it was time.

"Good luck, Jacky," Edwin said. "Let the fun begin."

I hit the start button on my watch and my treadmill, and I was off.

The early miles passed in a blur. I turned on the drama series *Dexter*—I'd eventually watch an entire season during this run. My dog Garnet stayed on the mat next to me for a while, watching me, perhaps wondering when I was going to pause and give her a treat. Edwin would pop in every few miles to see how I was doing, cross a few numbers off the whiteboard, and take a photo to post on Instagram stories. The kids would spend some time playing on the nearby yoga mats and telling me to run faster. While they were there, I switched the TV to *How to Train Your Dragon* and *Ice Age*, figuring that at seven and ten, they were a bit young for a show about serial killers (including one with the same name as my son!).

What the course lacked in scenery, it made up for in convenience. Edwin could easily refill the hydration bottles on either side of the treadmill display. Every few hours, I'd take a bathroom break, and occasionally I swapped out my sopping shirt for a new one. (The shorts, I kept the same; trying to balance on one leg to change out my bottoms just wasn't going to happen.) The strategy worked to keep me relatively fresh, at least for a while. In the photo of me at mile 32, I look downright perky. I'm glistening with sweat, despite the big fan set up next to the treadmill, but I have the energy to stick my tongue out in a cheeky greeting.

Once in the afternoon and once at about the halfway mark, I saw a smiling face appear in the window next to me. Rachel Zelibor and another friend, Lauren, had come to cheer me on in a socially distant fashion, and their presence was a welcome distraction.

Edwin snapped photos of them too, and I did my best to smile for the camera, though the fatigue was creeping up on me.

Besides being mentally exhausting, running on a treadmill is also far more physically taxing than outdoor running when it comes to how repetitive the movement is. Without the normal variations in terrain that you'd get even on a relatively flat road, on a treadmill each step pounds and rubs in the same way. And with upward of 150,000 steps in 100 miles, the impact and friction add up! Somewhere around mile 60, I started to feel the telltale burning of blisters on my stump. Between that pain and the mental tedium, I hit a wall and wasn't sure I could keep going.

The next time Edwin came in, I told him as much. "I'm struggling," I said. "And doesn't the treadmill seem to be close to burning out too?"

He walked to the front, inspecting the motor. "It's running a little hot, but I think it's okay," he said. "If *you* need a break, though, Jacky, why don't you take one? It's been a while since you've eaten anything besides gels and fruit chews."

So around mile 62—that's 100 kilometers—I devoured an entire pizza. A huge part of me wanted to declare it good enough and call it a day. "One hundred kilometers is impressive enough, right?" I asked Edwin. "I really don't want to get back on there."

Again, he assumed the role of a trusted crew member—one who knew me well enough to hold me accountable to my own goals and standards, and who knew that what I needed at that moment was some tough love.

"Jacky," he said, "everything you do is impressive. But I know you're strong enough to keep going. If you quit now, you're going to be so angry later on. With yourself, but also with me! We just can't have that."

I don't know if it was the snarky pep talk or the pepperoni—probably, it was a little bit of both—but with a fresh tank top and a fresh perspective, I got back on the moving belt and cruised far more smoothly for the next 15 miles.

From that point on, I knew deep down that I was going to be able to finish. Edwin stayed in the room as we counted down the final miles, marking them off on the whiteboard one at a time. We also switched up the TV again, this time, to *Formula 1: Drive to Survive*. It didn't matter much to me; I could barely concentrate on anything besides lifting each leg, one at a time, over and over.

Once we were down to the last mile, Edwin took the video live once again on Instagram. He kept me talking, both so I would stay awake and moving and so that the growing online audience would have something to listen to besides the whir of the treadmill belt.

"Do you know how to stand still on the ground without moving your legs?" he joked.

"Nope," I answered, chuckling.

By the end, I'm calling out each one-hundredth of a mile—99.9, 99.94, 99.96, 99.99… And then I lifted my hands in victory and, finally, it was done. In true runner fashion, I stopped my watch first and *then* stopped the treadmill, a move that made Edwin fear I would tumble off. "Stop that thing! Get off, get off!" he called out.

I complied, stepping off the belt and teetering on the edge of the treadmill frame as I turned to the camera. "I'm dead. But I've done it," I said. "And I did it in twenty-three hours, thirty-eight minutes." It was well within my twenty-four-hour goal. I gave my followers a double thumbs-up before Edwin stopped the video and came over to catch me, helping me sit down. I think he really didn't trust that I could stand on solid ground—and he was probably right!

As tired as I was, the moment was truly magical. I'd conquered what was by far the hardest thing I'd ever done. Edwin snapped a photo of me right then. I'm crouched over on the edge of the treadmill and appear exhausted, but my huge smile is genuine, beaming out my pride and my gratitude. When I look at it, I see someone who set out to achieve something huge, adapted the goal to meet the circumstances, and wound up with an entirely different, richer life than she ever would have imagined.

After a much-needed shower, a huge glass of wine, and a long nap, I scrolled back through the posts Edwin had made and all the comments viewers had left. I couldn't believe how many people had reshared my stories, tuned in to our livestreams, and offered words of encouragement. I knew it would take time to reply to everyone, but my goal was to acknowledge each and every person who reached out.

But before I could even make a dent, the number of messages began to increase exponentially. Soon, I realized why. A journalist from *Women's Health* magazine had been tuned in the whole time, and she wrote up a piece about my efforts. The magazine had even embedded some of our live video in the online story—something I was grateful for, because as a social media newbie at the time, I hadn't even thought to save it!

I was surprised and also thrilled—not because I wanted the personal glory (at this point, I think you know I have a love/hate relationship with attention) but because I had aspired to provide a bright spot in a time that was short on hope. I wanted my challenge to be a beacon of resilience that would encourage other amputees to push their boundaries and give everyone a reason to keep going. I hoped this extra exposure would help more people see it.

Once the *Women's Health* article went up, the story took off. While I'd done interviews and articles here and there before, this was by far the most media attention I'd ever received. My local ABC television station contacted me, as did *Canadian Running* magazine and several podcasts. In each interview, I emphasized that while what I was doing seemed extraordinary, it all began with a goal, some grit, and the willingness to adapt to changing circumstances. And anyone could follow in my footsteps, figuratively if not literally. "We all have the ability to do far more than we think," I kept saying.

Once again, I felt some of my self-doubt and fears about not belonging in the running world lift away. I'd truly believed there was a greater purpose to what I was doing, and that it would motivate all kinds of people to push boundaries and discover new possibilities. Now, it seemed, people were listening.

I uploaded my results to the Aravaipa Strong dashboard, and not long afterward, my wooden 100-mile belt buckle arrived. As I ran my fingers along the etched wording, I couldn't help but appreciate how things had turned out. Don't get me wrong—I wanted nothing more than for the pandemic to be over, or for it to have never begun in the first place. But especially given the circumstances, I was grateful my story could reach so many people. Had I run Umstead, it's unlikely my accomplishment would have gotten so much attention. I knew I wanted to continue using my running to tell a bigger story, and for that to happen, I needed to be flexible about writing, and rewriting, the next chapters.

Of course, all this started with me setting that big, hairy 100-mile goal in the first place. These types of plans and targets play a huge role in a competitive athlete's life. Without choosing goals to go after, we wouldn't know where to focus our efforts, or how much or what type of training to do. We also might lack the motivation needed to work hard enough to do our best.

But as famed martial artist and actor Bruce Lee said, "A goal is not always meant to be reached; it often serves simply as something to aim at." The most accomplished people don't achieve absolutely everything they set out to do. In fact, I'd argue that anyone with a 100 percent success rate probably isn't dreaming big enough. The key, I've found, is to set your goal and then stay open to the possibility that your achievements can take a different shape than you expect.

Sometimes that's a completely positive thing, such as when we notch one big victory and another door opens for us. But honestly, most of the time, it involves bouncing back from a disappointment, whether that's a canceled race, a performance that isn't what we'd hoped, or even a life-altering illness or injury. The longer I run, the more I learn to take all these situations in stride. Yes, I might throw a pity party, but it's much easier than ever to pick up the pieces.

That doesn't mean you have to be happy about what happened, especially at first, although eventually you may come to see the positive outcomes of even your darkest days. However, it does mean you can't get stuck in the should-haves or other negative emotions, or let them cloud your thinking. You need a clear understanding of where you are so you can plan how best to move forward.

~

The entire year of 2023 brought this idea home for me in a way few other time periods had. I kicked things off at Across the Years, finally earning that 200-mile belt buckle that had previously eluded me. But remember, that was a pivot from my original goal of achieving that distance at the Moab 240, a race I had signed up for twice but failed to finish the first time and then didn't even start the second time. After the success at Across the Years, though, many of my other big goals for 2023 didn't pan out the way I'd planned.

First, there was my do-over attempt at the Umstead 100 in April. Training was tough enough on its own, and then right as I was ramping up, an accident with boiling water caused a second-degree burn on my leg, which made running painful. After it healed and I was able to run again, I got sick and unintentionally lost weight. As soon as I felt better, my kids got sick, meaning I spent a lot of time in nurse mode and not nearly as much time as I'd have liked out on the trails.

On race morning, I showed up as best I could. Even though I'd recruited an amazing crew, that was the race where my weight loss led to extra chafing between my liner and my blade, causing me to DNF after mile 75. And then I posted yet another DNF, at the Yeti 100-miler in September, after all that drama with the threatening man beside the trail had thrown me off pace.

Yet those weren't the moments that defined the year for me. In the midst of those so-called failures were so many highlights. I was named both the Road Runners Club of America Adaptive Athlete of the Year and the Amputee Blade Runners Athlete of the Year. I ran my fastest mile ever—a 5:33—and racked up a grand total of more than 3,000 miles throughout the twelve months. I finished the 100K at the Javelina Jundred and logged more than 150 half marathons for Project "I Can Do Hard Things," which continued on into January. I even became a certified scuba diver thanks to my partnership with Garmin—another thing I never would have expected running to bring into my life!

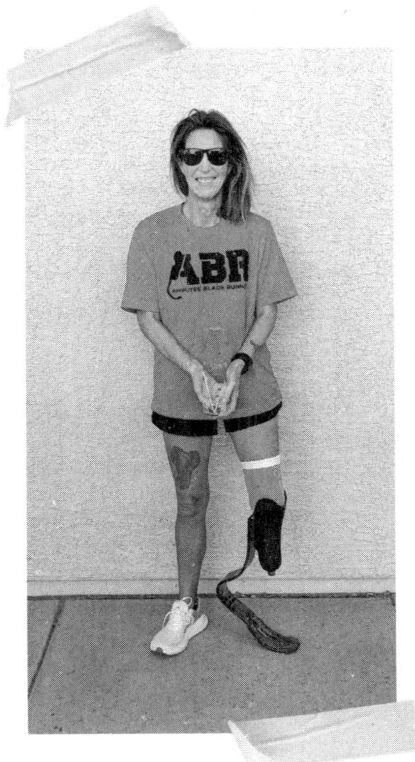

Yes, I had lots of big goals when I started the year. Some of them, I knocked out of the park. Others knocked me down on my rear—yet more times I had to bum-shuffle when I wasn't intending to. But every time, I got back up and set new goals, many of which were things I couldn't even have conceived of achieving when the clock struck midnight during the Across the Years race. If I hadn't been able to adjust, I'd have missed out on all the upsides.

There's a sentiment I like that's usually attributed to Winston Churchill: "Success isn't final, and failure isn't fatal." I don't know if he's actually the one who said it, but regardless, the meaning rings true. When you look closely at anyone's journey, even those who seem to have achieved the most, you'll see an endless ebb and flow of high points and low ones. Study the patterns even more intently and you'll likely find that many of the greatest successes come after what feels like a setback or even a breakdown. In other words, adapting to new circumstances isn't a deviation from your path toward greater things, it's an essential part of the process. Take it from one of the greatest tennis players of all time, Roger Federer, an eight-time Wimbledon champion. In a commencement speech on June 9, 2024, at Dartmouth College, he shared that he'd won almost 80 percent of the more than fifteen hundred matches he'd played in his career. Then he asked the audience: "What percentage of points do you think I won during those matches?"

The answer? Just 54 percent, meaning one of the best players in the world lost nearly *half* the points across matches. "When you lose nearly every second point on average," he said, "you learn not to dwell on every shot."

When I'm tempted to let a defeat or a detour define me, I allow myself space for the pity party, then take a pause and reflect. I ask myself what's changed and how I can adapt my goals and strategies in kind. Can I pursue the same goal on a different course or at a later date? Or can I tweak the goal, potentially even making it more ambitious? Maybe—as with the treadmill 100-miler—I can create my own opportunities entirely.

If I'm still feeling down, I remind myself of all the ways unexpected detours have led to even more exciting and rewarding adventures. I recall the extra miles I ran at the Speed Project and how, in the end, they took nothing away from the finish. I think about my DNFs at Umstead and Yeti, and how they inspired me to start Project "I Can Do Hard Things." I remember that I probably never would have started running at all were it not for my cancer and amputation! And then, I think back on the shifting goalposts of the marathon record, with gratitude.

Marathon 103 of 104

Thanks to my final fundraising push, I secured a total of $88,000 in a single weekend. And then, on a Zoom call a few days later, my RXBAR contacts surprised me with even more good news. Though I hadn't quite reached the $104,000 to get the match, they were still donating the full amount, bringing my grand total to nearly $200,000. That meant about twenty athletes would receive new blades from Amputee Blade Runners, all because I stayed flexible instead of cracking.

14

STAY TRUE TO YOU

Marathon 104 of 104

Saturday, April 30, 2022. The last of my 104 days of adventure was finally here. I had friends planning to join me in the later miles. A fifteen-minute drive away from Veterans Oasis Park, at the Four Silos Brewery, a T-shirt and an ice-cold draft beer waited for me.

As I started on the first dusty loop on my own, the park was quiet around me except for the gentle cooing of mourning doves and the cackling of grackles. I listened to the thunk of my blade in the dirt, my mind drifting back to the beginning of my running journey. When I first heard that sound, I hated it; I thought I sounded like a pirate with a wooden leg. But now, as I note the subtle differences between my right and left steps, I hear something entirely different. "Strength," my stride says. "Dedication." "Gratitude."

I'd been running at least four hours for so many days, and now that was about to be over. As I continued for the first lap, then the second and third, an internal tug-of-war started happening inside me. On the one hand, I was tired and ready to stop. The swelling in my stump might finally subside. There was a chance I could go back to a full night's sleep, rather than being kept awake by cramps and nerve pain. I could once again chaperone a school trip or take a weekend family getaway without stressing over when to squeeze in 26.2 miles.

Yet as excited as I felt about all these upsides, a sense of sadness came over me too. For more than three months, this quest had dominated my life. Despite the challenges, there was something so simple about my mission and the structure it brought to my days. Get up, get the kids out the door, eat, run, eat again, recover, eat some more, then repeat. It was hard to contemplate what I'd do with all my hours otherwise.

And then there was the competitive fire inside me. At this point, I had surpassed my goal and, as far as I knew, set an official Guinness World Record. I was no longer worried about whether I'd finish; I'd already overachieved. But a voice inside of me wondered, instead, could I keep going even farther? And should I? Had I truly reached the limits of my potential, or were there even more marathons within me, just waiting to be tapped?

By the last two loops, when a handful of my local running buddies joined me, I honestly hadn't decided whether to stop at 104 or keep going. "Don't worry about it right now, Jacky," I told myself. "Enjoy these miles with your friends. You can decide tonight."

There were about ten of us running together as we rounded the final bend toward the parking lot. I dropped back for a bit so I could look around with gratitude at everyone who had come to support me. A local runner who saw me on the news was there with her ten-year-old daughter, and as they ran together and smiled, my heart warmed. Then there was another mom from a nearby running group, and as I watched her take a sip from her water bottle, I felt a wave of sadness. Her teenage daughter had passed away from cancer just a couple of years prior.

She'd told me before that she found hope in my journey as a survivor. Seeing her on this run, I couldn't help but consider how short life could be, how precious the moments with our families were. I thought of Dexter and Eliza, and Edwin too. As much as this multimarathon quest had streamlined my life, it undoubtedly made theirs a bit more complicated. They hadn't complained or questioned me but steadfastly supported me. Everyone picked up extra chores, Edwin adjusted his own running schedule, and the kids looked for homework help elsewhere, knowing that Mummy's fatigued brain could *not* handle middle-school math.

This time, as we wrapped up the 26.2, there was no tape or dramatic finish-line flourish. Edwin snapped a photo of the group, we exchanged sweaty hugs and high fives, and then we divided up to drive over to Four Silos. I didn't even bother to change out of my running blade before I slid into the passenger seat. As I sat there, I took a deep breath and I knew: It was over. I *could* keep going to 105 and beyond, yes. But *should*, and *would*, those were different matters.

Running had transformed me, but it didn't define me. I was still all the other things I had been before the challenge—a wife, a mom, a classroom helper, a dog owner, a full-fledged human. The sport had become a critical part of my life, but it wasn't all I was. For a period of time, I'd tilted the balance to accomplish a specific goal, and that was okay—admirable, even. Now that I'd done what I'd set out to do, though, it was time to right the ship and restore the symmetry.

Whether it's in running, parenthood, your career, or another aspect of life, there are times when chasing huge goals—or coping with major crises—requires an almost single-minded focus. When you first have a new baby, for instance, it takes all your time and energy to feed and soothe them. Before a big presentation at work, you might burn the midnight oil in preparation. In the aftermath of something like a cancer diagnosis, your world shrinks as you channel everything into survival.

But your target race will come and go, whether you achieve your time goal or cross the finish line or not. Kids grow bigger and more self-sufficient, going to school and, eventually, making lives of their own. You'll knock that slide show out of the park and land a new client, or maybe you'll make some mistakes, but either way, you'll come home to your garden or your pets or your partner. If you're fortunate enough for your cancer treatments to be successful, you'll realize there's life on the other side, a new normal to navigate.

I say it all the time, and I'll say it again: We're all capable of so much more than we think. Our greatest highs can be beyond our wildest dreams, and when the chips are down, we can cope with far more than we ever knew possible. But sometimes the key to doing any of this is knowing when it's time to scale back, shift gears, or let go. As much as I encourage everyone to dream big and chase adventure, it's important not to lose the essence of ourselves in the process.

I've always laughed at the idea of "having it all." Yes, you can be a parent and a successful career person and a top athlete and a loving spouse—but you can't give everyone and everything your all, every hour of every day. Depending on your season of life and the demands you're dealing with, it makes sense that you'd prioritize some areas over others some of the time.

The key to making a big, audacious life work over the long term is to keep checking in and evaluating your equilibrium. Sometimes, that means sitting down in the days after you achieve something huge and thinking about how to rebalance all your life buckets. In other cases, it's taking breaks during an intense period when you're a bit off-kilter to give something or someone else you care about some extra attention. Even if you do, though, difficult choices may still emerge along the way—judgment calls that test your values and your identity.

~

October 2020

From the moment I heard about the Moab 240, the event had been on my must-do list. The single, giant loop starts and ends in Moab,

Utah, a town of about five thousand people that serves as a gateway to stunning Arches National Park. Along the way, runners pass through red-rock canyons and over peaks in two separate mountain ranges, climbing and ascending a total of about 30,000 feet.

Even the backstory of the race was compelling to me. A Utah ultrarunner named Stephen Jones first conceived of a 200-mile course in this area and suggested it to his friend Candice Burt, who owns a company called Destination Trail. "Two hundred is the new one hundred," Stephen was fond of saying, noting that runners were always looking for the next big challenge. He believed they'd flock to a long race in this landscape. Candice listened, but she had too many other things on her plate to look into the idea at the time.

In 2016, not long after he proposed this idea, Stephen tragically passed away in an avalanche while skiing. Mourning her friend, Candice finally explored the Moab area and found it breathtaking. She realized Stephen had been right about its potential for a long race, and she revisited the course he'd sent her and fine-tuned it. In doing so, she also found that, due to the terrain, it couldn't even be contained to 200 miles (240 is the new 200, I guess!). The following year, 2017, the first runners lined up. "It's really quite an adventure of the physical variety, and spiritual, and mental," Candice explains in a video on the Destination Trail website. "Runners will experience a little bit of everything."

Like many other events of this type and duration, the Moab 240 is not even considered a race; officially, it's an endurance run. Yes, times are recorded and top finishers receive awards, and, in fact, one of the things that had drawn me in was that Courtney Dauwalter, one of my ultrarunning idols, had won the event outright that first year, beating all the women *and* all the men. Though the course limit is 112 hours, she finished in 57 hours, 55 minutes, and 13 seconds—an incredible *10 hours* ahead of the second-place finisher. But for most of the runners out there, it's about the experience, not trying to get the fastest time.

Due to its remote location, the race was able to go on in 2020 when so many others were canceled due to COVID restrictions, and I followed it obsessively online. The winner, an Italian American former model named Michele Graglia, ran a time of 61 hours, 43 minutes, and 15 seconds, despite injuring his Achilles tendon between the 200- and 210-mile mark. If you want an idea of how gnarly this course is, former Navy SEAL and author David Goggins, who's famously hardcore, came in second, nearly 1 hour and 40 minutes behind Graglia. Tracking the elites was exciting, but what I loved most was how many other types of runners streamed through the finish line after them—athletes of all levels and body shapes, smiling, whooping, and even breaking down into emotional tears as they did so.

The challenge thrilled me, and the videos and images floored me. I saw the stunning views from the peaks that were surrounded by aspens in bright fall colors, looking out upon rivers and gorges. Runners strode down desert roads that seemed to stretch into infinity as sunrises and sunsets appeared over rust-colored rock formations. "I have to do this," I thought, as I scrolled.

At the time, I'd only just completed my first 100-miler, and that was on the treadmill. Doing the math, though, made a race of more than double the distance seem less intimidating—112 hours was four and a half days, meaning you'd only have to do 60 miles a day. Plus, you could take breaks to eat and even to sleep. Five of the aid stations had tents and cots, and you could also nap in your crew members' cars, or even out under the stars on the trail. When registration opened for 2021, I signed up.

Only then, as usual, did I break the news to Edwin. "I've signed up for a 240-mile race," I told him at dinner that night. His eyes widened and he took a breath, opening his mouth to say something, but I stopped him. "I have four days to finish it—I can totally do that! You and the kids can come too. It'll be an adventure!"

He closed his mouth again and smiled, shaking his head ever so slightly. "All right, Jacky," he said. "I guess you've found your next mission."

Then, I told my Instagram followers: "I will be running Moab 240 in October. Yes, that's running 240 miles—just over nine marathons, back-to-back—in the desert on a prosthetic leg all at once. What could possibly go wrong?" Now I just needed to find a crew and figure out how to train for a 240-mile foot race.

~

In some ways, I already knew how to prepare: doing what I was already doing, just more of it. By this point, I'd fully embraced the idea that power hiking was a part of ultrarunning, and so I didn't hesitate to incorporate it into my training. I'd even added some lettering to the side of my walking socket that said "Ultra Runner," to make it all seem more official and intentional!

In total, I ran or walked four to six days a week, mixing up recovery runs, vertical runs, power hikes, and long runs. Often I'd wear a weighted vest to build up core strength. That was important because I knew I'd have to carry gloves, warm clothes, and at least three liters of water with me in the race. We could put some of our gear in drop bags that would be driven to the sixteen aid stations, and about half of those stops were also accessible to our crew, who could bring us more supplies. But some aid stations were as many as 20 miles apart. We'd have to carry a lot of what we needed on our backs.

Some weekends, I'd do back-to-back long runs—say, six hours on a Friday night, five hours on Saturday morning, and another three hours later in the day. That gave me experience in running at night and completing long distances on tired legs. At first, I was afraid to run in the dark. I already couldn't completely feel the ground beneath my feet, so losing sight of what was ahead felt intimidating. Eventually, though, I came to find it extremely relaxing. I simply have to focus on what's directly in front of me, and I become grounded and centered.

That type of compartmentalizing doesn't come easily these days. We all have tiny computers in our pockets and can be reached—or reach out ourselves—at every hour of the day. Though it's somewhat counterintuitive, I think tuning out from time to time is another key to living a well-balanced life. When I'm on the trail, I do my best to stay fully immersed in where I am, soaking up every moment of bliss. When I'm in family mode, I try to be just as present for my kids and partner. That type of focus can be a superpower, if you let it. When the time you spend on any person or pursuit is high-quality, rather than scattered and halfhearted, each hour and day instantly feels more whole and expansive.

This sense of presence was especially helpful during my Moab build, since, as you can tell, I spent a lot of time running! Edwin, ever the supportive crew member, committed to my mission too. We worked together to stagger our training and make sure the household and kids were taken care of. My plan called for increasing distance and intensity for two weeks, and then I'd have a recovery week, with a decrease in mileage. During those lighter days, I'd spend more time with Dexter and Eliza and catch up on tasks around the house. Together, we all found a balance that worked for us.

Of course, almost as soon as we did, we had to make some more adjustments. Edwin had changed jobs in November, and by June they had offered him the chance to relocate to the Phoenix area. After five years in North Carolina, we were ready to try something new—that call to adventure, all over again! But coordinating a nearly cross-country relocation, with two kids in school, wasn't an easy feat.

Once we arrived in Arizona, though, things began falling into place again. The kids quickly grew to love their new school and their new neighborhood in suburban Gilbert. We were so much closer to the trails here, including the San Tan Mountains, full of rocky terrain that was similar to what I'd see in Utah. Sometimes I'd get to a plateau or a peak and pause, marveling at the beauty of the majestic saguaros and the layered mesas in the distance. Yes, it was hot, but at least we'd escaped the humidity of North Carolina.

As the dust settled—literally and figuratively—I took stock. "Yes," I thought. "This place feels right for all of us."

~

By September, I'd worked my way up to eleven-hour training sessions, alternating power hiking at a pace of 14 minutes per mile and easy running at a 10- to 12-minute pace. All my 40-percent-incline treadmill hikes and rocky, sweaty trail runs brought me confidence. But as October neared, some anxiety crept in. I'd never trained as hard for anything as I had for this. I knew I was ready, but having had such a huge goal for so long made the stakes feel higher than before.

This was also the first time I'd gone into a race with a small bit of a spotlight on me. I had so many more social media followers now than I did before my treadmill 100-miler. I'd done interviews beforehand too, and even written a couple of columns for *Trail Runner* magazine about my preparation and goals. The pressure might have been mostly self-imposed, but I still felt the weight of others' expectations, and the sense that I didn't want to let down other amputees or anyone who'd supported or invested in me.

All this swirled in my mind as I put the finishing touches on the logistics. I lined up pacers and crew, including Edwin and my brother, Lionel, and arranged to take the kids out of their new school for a bit. I decided which of my several running legs and walking feet to take with us, and, of course, I made sure I had several rolls of my trusty duct tape. Soon, it was time to make the seven-and-a-half-hour drive.

The thing about the desert and mountains in October is that you never quite know what conditions you're going to get. In 2020, when I was following along with this event online, the weather was dry and hot as heck. This year was a totally different scene. By the time we'd arrived in Moab, heavier-than-normal rains had turned the course muddy and slick. "Just my luck," I told Edwin the day beforehand. "Rain, again."

To make matters worse, snow and severe wind gusts threatened to make running up the mountains too dangerous. Up until the race began, there were murmurs that it might not take place at all. In the end, they rerouted the later part of the course—after about mile 150—around the second of the two peaks, avoiding the riskiest sections.

But as I stood on the starting line at 6:00 a.m., that was all ahead of me. The sun wouldn't rise for another hour, so about 175 of us took off into the dark, leaving the cheers of the crowd and the flashbulbs of photographers behind to chase our headlamps into the desert ahead of us. I'd prepared as well as I could without allowing my life to be consumed by my efforts. All I could do now was my best.

After 3 flat miles through town, the next 7 included about 1,000 feet of climbing. For me, though, things were going downhill quickly. As the sun rose, it revealed a gray, cloudy sky that quickly began to release a drizzle, then a steady shower. I once again found myself battling my trail nemesis: mud. Unlike in my earlier muddy races, such as Triple Lakes, I now had multiple options of feet and blades to choose from to help me power through. Still, the conditions slowed me down and forced me to focus on the ground even more than I usually would.

That's why, as I made my way to my first meetup with Edwin and the rest of my crew near mile 18, I did something else I've done before—I went off course. At one point, several other runners and I were supposed to go straight. But because the drizzle was in our eyes and I was staring down so as not to lose my footing, we missed the markers and turned right instead. From there, we got turned in circles for a bit, trying to find our way back to the trail. I did my best to stay calm and follow along, but in the end, we probably lost about half an hour to the error.

Still, I tried my best to smile as I pulled into the aid station a few minutes later. Honestly, it wasn't too tough to look happy; seeing Edwin, Lionel, and the kids gave me an instant mood boost.

"I got lost for a bit, but I found myself," I told Edwin after a soggy hug. "I still feel okay, but I'm a little worried about the next section." I knew there'd be some climbing—and even worse, an incredibly steep descent—on a section with plenty of slickrock, the name for a surface polished smooth by centuries of wind and rain.

The slickrock I'd already encountered was even, well, slicker than usual in the rain. I debated the choice of what foot to use, unsure which would give me the best traction. In the end, I went with my walking foot, figuring that the tread on the heavy-duty trail shoes I was wearing was more rugged than the one on my blade.

About six and a half miles later, I made a slight right on the trail to get to the notorious section of the course known as Jacob's Ladder, nearly a half mile of descent on "steps" made of slickrock. And as soon as I felt the ground, I regretted my gear choice. Yes, power hiking is a part of my training, but to be honest, on the most technical trails, I'm far more confident on my blade than on my walking foot. Fear gripped me as I peered down. (Remember, I'm scared of heights!) I even sat for a moment on one of the wide, flat rocks. "How will I get myself to the bottom of this insane trail?" I wondered.

Eventually, I picked my way down, but I was far slower than I wanted to be, especially considering the time I'd already lost. At that point, as darkness began to fall, I caught up with two other runners, a man and a woman. Excited to have company—and fearing that I'd get lost again—I stuck with them, even though they were going at a slower pace than I'd been traveling.

We talked a bit about our hometowns—one was from Texas, the other from Florida—and the struggles the rain had added to an already challenging day. I noticed the woman was a lot chattier. In fact, the man wasn't looking so great. He could barely keep his eyes open as he struggled to push forward. We even paused so he could take a ten-minute trail nap, but when he awoke, he was still quite wobbly. I had visions of him tumbling right off the side of the mesa. I also had a strong suspicion that we were at the back of the pack and that no other runners would be coming through. Even if he simply stepped off the trail and went to sleep for longer, I wasn't sure how long it would be before someone else would come by to find him.

My inner self-talk grew conflicted. "If I were by myself, I would be running faster," I thought. "But I can't leave. What if something were to happen to him? I couldn't live with myself." It felt like a battle between my athletic, striving self and my human, caring side.

In the end, it really wasn't a question; I was always going to stay. As we arrived at the Oasis aid station at mile 57.2, a volunteer—a friend of mine named Wes—greeted me. As soon as I saw him, my heart sank. I realized what his job was, and that he wasn't happy about doing it. "I'm getting cut off, aren't I?" I asked him. He looked down, then nodded, ever so slightly. "Yeah," he said quietly. We'd missed the cutoff time by just 6 minutes. I burst into tears, and as I sobbed, he hugged me.

I won't lie: I'd had a few DNFs already by this point, including my 100-miler at Umstead just the previous spring, but this one really stung. After all the buildup, the weeks and months of hard work, and the splash of publicity, I felt embarrassed and frustrated. Given everyone who was tracking me, I knew I had to make a public post with an at least somewhat positive spin, and I tried my best.

Inside, though, my pity party was raging. I second-guessed everything, most especially my wrong turn and my decision to tackle Jacob's Ladder on my walking foot.

Edwin had been tracking my progress from the Indian Creek aid station at mile 72.5, which I never reached. "Jacky," he asked me later, when we reunited, "what happened? You were right on pace until you reached those other two runners. Then you totally slowed down."

I sighed, pushing back tears. "I know," I said. "But I didn't want to leave anyone behind. This community has come through for me so many times. I had to return the favor."

And as I reflected on it, that choice—to stay with the struggling runner and see him through to the aid station—was the one thing I wasn't doubting. If faced with the identical circumstances all over again, I would have 100 percent taken the same action. No finish line matters more than the type of person I am and the example I set for my children.

Dexter and Eliza were proud of me no matter what. Honestly, they were just happy to be excused from school to take a big, exciting trip to a different desert and mountain range. And when I told them the story, I could see they were both inspired by my big goals but also understanding of why I'd forgo them. Leaving someone behind and in danger simply wasn't an option.

At first, I shuddered to scroll through the comments on my DNF post. Once I finally did, I realized that others saw my efforts in a similar light—not as a knock on my athletic abilities but as a demonstration of the broader spirit of the sport. "Your strength and perseverance are incredible," one person posted. "That man was lucky to have you by his side." Another commented: "One of my trail friends loves to use the phrase indomitable spirit. That is you. Keep inspiring us all." Some nearly brought me to tears all over again: "Do you realize you're our hero already, that you won before you officially started?"

~

We all face these turning points and tests in our lives, times when we must choose between two paths that often feel equally slippery or rocky. At certain junctures, it can seem like we have to choose between our roles and identities. Do we make this call as a parent or as a professional? An athlete or a caregiver? A partner or a competitor?

Oftentimes, there's no single right answer. Every option can involve trade-offs. Doing the "right" thing in one domain can mean neglecting another, at least for a few miles.

Deep down, I've found there's usually a small inner voice that guides us toward the best balance for each of us. Some might call it a conscience, a soul, or a value system. It might be instilled by parents and other loved ones, or arise from a religious background, or simply develop over time into a deeply held conviction about what's truly important to us.

In my experience, if you're listening closely enough to hear it, you'll worry less about what strangers think of you and more about the way you want to show up in the world and for those closest to you. Like I said in the last chapter, it also involves being willing to adapt to new information and circumstances and adjust your goals accordingly. And you can also try the mental exercise I turned to during Moab. If I made this choice, how would I feel about myself the day after?

Sometimes, that voice doesn't become clear until after you've decided or taken an action. Once you head down a certain path, you might realize that it doesn't truly align with where you want to wind up. And that's okay too. As I've found time and again during races, there's always an opportunity to course-correct and get back on the proper route.

Marathon 104 of 104

Fast-forward a few years from Moab to the day I finished marathon 104. As we reconvened at Four Silos, I slowly savored one of the brewery's ice-cold creations. The alcohol went straight to my head after so many days of sweating in the hot sun, drinking only water and Tailwind sports drinks. True to his word, the owner, Mike, presented me with a yellow T-shirt that said "104 Marathons" on the front, next to the Four Silos logo. "All of Gilbert is so proud of you, Jacky!" he said.

As we lingered on the patio, staying in the shade as best we could, a sleepy sense of satisfaction drifted over me. Eliza set down her root beer and came over to hug me. "This was so fun, Mummy," she said. "But you're done now, right?"

I held her close to my side and kissed the top of her head. "Yes, kiddo," I said. "We did it, and now it's over. Tomorrow, I rest."

15

TELL YOUR STORY

1 Day After Marathon 104 of 104

I opened my eyes, slowly, on May 1. It was morning and time to get up and get the kids off to school. After they left, I *wasn't* going for a run—for the first time in three and a half months.

To say it felt odd would be an understatement. At this point, my body expected to get ready, then hit the pavement, trail, or treadmill. I wasn't exactly sure what, or when, to eat. I didn't even really know what to wear; for so long, I'd been existing only in running clothes!

I joked on Instagram that I was planning to set a record for the most consecutive rest days. The truth is, even though I was planning to take a full two-week break from running, I had plenty of things to keep me busy.

One major task was to complete all the paperwork required to secure my Guinness World Record. To be honest, this was only slightly less daunting than running the miles had been. I had to upload each run as a separate GPS file, along with photos taken at the beginning, middle, and end. Then, I gathered up all the statements from witnesses to attest that they saw me doing all my runs. I understood why they needed so much detail to verify all my efforts, but it was certainly a lot of work.

And then, there was the media.

The story of my marathon record attempt had already been in the running press—I'd done interviews with *Runner's World* magazine, *Women's Running*, the *Ali on the Run* podcast, *Canadian Running*, and more. As the final days neared, mainstream publications and shows started to take notice too.

When I was still doing a marathon a day, I'd been scheduling Zoom calls with reporters in the afternoons and evenings, apologizing for my fatigue after a long day of running. I even did an interview from a hotel treadmill the day after the Boston Marathon. Once I achieved my goal, the story further exploded and I had even more requests: ESPN, BBC, *People* magazine, *Access Hollywood*, and NPR's *Morning Edition* covered my project. I was even in the German newspaper *Die Welt* and on TV as far away as Australia! By now, millions of people across the country and around the world were learning about what I had done.

The attention was still a bit strange for me, but on the other side of my accomplishment, I felt more confident than ever in my message. In a way, it was like I'd discovered a secret about how to transform your mindset and your life, and now I was being given the opportunity to share it far and wide. Running these 104 (or, really, 105) marathons had allowed me to *show* and not just *tell* it, and divulging the behind-the-scenes details, I knew, also made the message hit home even more.

I talked about the moments I wanted to quit but didn't. I went through the challenges I'd faced, including the way my stump swelled, causing me to switch to an older running blade, one I desperately hoped wouldn't snap in the middle of a marathon. I described the nighttime cramps, the fueling mishaps, the shifting goalposts, the dreadful day of not just one but two 26.2-mile journeys back-to-back.

I also shared the beautiful parts: The friends and supporters who showed up for me, both in person and virtually. The students at my kids' school, who waved to me every time I circled by, again and again and again. When I finished, they awarded me a homemade banner that said "Congrats, Mrs. Broersma!" Each one had signed their name and written a personal message too; Eliza's said, "You are the best mom ever." I described everything from the honor of running the Boston Marathon in the para division to the joy I got from watching silly movies and TV shows during my treadmill runs.

I told reporters how I'd focused on the good to get through the tough, one day and even one mile at a time.

Over and over again, I made clear that while not everyone would choose this particular type of challenge, anyone could learn from my example. "When I started, I had no idea if I could actually do this," I said. "Now, I'm here to tell everyone: You're capable of so much more than you think."

~

The finish line can feel like the dramatic conclusion to an epic adventure, but any runner can tell you the story doesn't end there. The conclusion of my marathon project was no exception. For weeks and even months after day 104, the ups and downs continued.

In June, two Scottish women who'd set out to break the record not long after I did reached 106 marathons. I'd been chatting with them all along as we encouraged each other, and I was happy for them to have reached their own massive goal, messaging them to say congratulations. Then all three of us got a surprise. We learned that another British runner who'd started around the same time as I had—and who'd planned to stop at 100 or 101—kept going until 106 too.

Alongside my joy at the accomplishments of these other amazing female athletes came a minor pang of regret that I hadn't extended my streak for a few more days. I let myself have a pity party, for a bit. But then, once I allowed myself to mourn the what-ifs, I felt at peace. I knew I'd made the best call I could with the information I had at the time, and it was the choice that was right for me and for my family. I also felt proud that we were all so close to the same number, given that I was the only one who was running with a prosthetic. It felt great to be able to compete with athletes without disabilities.

Besides, you know how I talked before about adapting your goals? Sometimes you work hard to do that yourself. In other cases, the universe conspires to give you a helping hand.

All of us record-chasers submitted our paperwork to Guinness, and we were each recognized. The British runner received the record for the most consecutive days to run a marathon distance, combining treadmill and outdoor runs. The Scottish runners claimed the record for the most consecutive days to run a marathon distance, outdoor only. My record, just two marathons shy of theirs, was for adaptive athletes.

When I got the email confirming the honor, I cried. I tell people all the time that the record wasn't really the goal—the whole thing was about pushing my limits and encouraging others to do the same. Still, seeing it in writing made it real and indisputable. I had set out to do this very hard thing, and I had done it. Even if the record eventually falls, as most do, no one can take this moment away from me.

The news coverage continued after the record became official. As I told my story, and read over the articles as they came out, I could scarcely believe all that my body had allowed me to accomplish. I also noticed that something was different compared to the stories that had been written about me in the past. More of them than ever included the word "athlete," and they often expressed astonishment that anyone, of any ability level, could do what I had done.

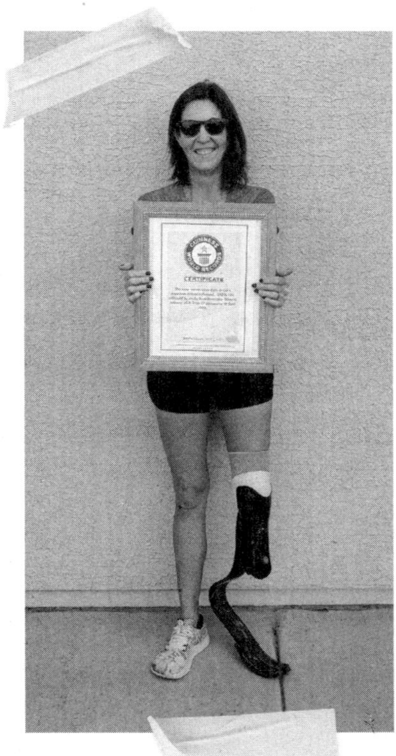

Yes, the articles, anchors,

and hosts talked about my amputation and my running blade—as they should, since it's an important part of my story. My own experiences and the information about my fundraising brought much-needed awareness to the cost of prosthetics and other challenges adaptive athletes often face.

Yet it was clear that what I had done transcended any labels. That box I felt I'd been put in years ago, when I first had my surgery? It finally began to dawn on me that not only had I climbed out of it, I'd smashed it behind me, so others could follow in my footsteps.

Before long, I'd have even more valuable evidence of this. For a few years, I'd been a member of something called the Altra Red Team. This was essentially an ambassador program for everyday athletes put together by the brand that makes my favorite trail-running footwear. In exchange for free shoes, swag, and discounts on other gear, I agreed to volunteer at Altra-sponsored events, wear my Red Team uniform at races, and talk about Altra on social media.

That all came naturally to me. After trying lots of different shoes, I came to love the way Altras fit and performed on the trails, and I had no problem talking up their gear and tagging them in my posts. Races were where I preferred to spend my free time anyway. As far as brand relationships go, it was as authentic as they come.

As my running journey continued, Altra became an even more trusted partner. During the 104-marathon journey, they provided me with extra shoes, which was very helpful, because, in those three months alone, I went through ten pairs! They also teamed with a producer to make a video about my Boston Marathon experience that I thought beautifully captured my story and my journey.

Through the years, I'd also gotten to know more of the professional trail runners with Altra. As part of the Elite Team, they had sponsorships at a higher level, complete with financial backing as well as gear. I remember chatting with one of them at a camp put on by the endurance sports app and community Strava. "Jacky, you really should be on the Elite Team with us," he told me.

At the time, I thought he was a bit off his rocker. That type of thing—being a sponsored, professional athlete—wasn't on my radar. Though I was building my endurance and extending my distances, I hadn't seen a runner who looked like me on any elite team. I didn't quite yet have the confidence to be a trailblazer in that way.

Behind the scenes, several athletes on the team went to bat for me, mentioning my accolades to the brand's sponsorship team. The fall after I completed my marathon record, Altra invited me to the Running Event, an annual industry gathering where brands, athletes, specialty stores, and running media all meet up. There, we discussed where my career was headed and what the brand was looking for—someone who wasn't afraid to do huge things on the trails, and to talk about it along the way. They shared some of the ways they envisioned supporting me, including working with me on a unique trail tread for my blade.

A few months later, in March of 2023, I signed a contract.

Words couldn't even begin to describe how excited I was. As a kid hiding in the bathroom during gym class, or even as a woman huffing and bleeding my way through that first 5K, I never could have imagined that I'd become a professional athlete years later. I thought about twenty-six-year-old Jacky, staring down at her legs in the bath the night before surgery or lying in her hospital bed in the days afterward. What if she could have known that—like Olympic and Paralympic swimmer Natalie du Toit in the news clipping on her wall—she'd go on to an athletic career that surpassed anything she dreamed of before her amputation?

Things might have been a lot easier for me if I could have foreseen the outcome. Yet, deep down, I knew that forging ahead into unknown adventures wasn't supposed to be easy. My scars, my highs and lows, the metal and carbon fiber in my blade—all of it was essential to the athlete and the person I'd become. There are parts of my journey I'd never choose to relive or wish on anyone else, but in the end, they're mine, and I'm grateful.

~

I can't go back in time and tell younger Jacky the victories that lie ahead, or any of the other things I'd want to share with her, which is mostly that everything is going to be okay and that she's stronger than she thinks. She wouldn't have believed me anyway. Both as a young girl and after my amputation, I was so focused on my so-called flaws that I couldn't comprehend they would wind up becoming my greatest strengths, or that every loss would eventually bring its own gifts.

I'd spent a good chunk of my childhood and fourteen of the years after my surgery trying my hardest to be happy while denying who I really was. In many ways, I regret those lost years, when the disconnect between my true self and how I presented to the world made me unhappier than ever. Yet I know that those struggles, too, were a chapter in my story, leading me to where I am today.

Since I can't change the past, my greatest hope is to shape the future. I want to teach my kids, and especially my daughter, not to spend their lives worrying about others' perceptions and to instead stay true to themselves. Girls and women in particular are given so many messages from society and mass media about how they should look and behave. But I've learned that happiness only comes when you break free and accept who you are instead of trying to meet those ever-changing, external ideals.

I see Eliza's beautiful inner spark every day, and I try my best to nurture it. Starting from the moment she put on her pink tutu and joined me for my first-ever run with a blade, she's been by my side for so much of my running journey. That morning, we just went about a block. But a bit later, when she was four years old, she said, "Mummy, I want to run with you." From then on, Sunday became our day to run together. I never pushed her on pace or distance, letting her decide how far and fast she wanted to go. We started with a few blocks, then worked our way to a mile, then a mile and a half.

By age five, she was up to 3 miles on the road. At six, she joined me on the trails, fearlessly bounding down hills and crossing streams. She smiled the whole time, and as I rushed to keep up with her, I smiled too.

When she was little, she'd demand we wear the same outfit while running, down to the sunglasses and headbands. Once, she put on one of my compression sleeves to go to preschool—yes, just one, since I usually only wear one on my right leg. When I was doing the 104 marathons, she'd bounce out of bed early on weekends and come to jog beside me for a few miles in her pajamas.

Of all the hours I spent circling my neighborhood or Veterans Oasis Park, those with Eliza were my favorites. She'd constantly entertain me, singing silly songs and telling me stories about her classmates and the plotlines of her favorite TV shows. I loved that she didn't care at all what people might think of her striding down the sidewalk in her pink flannel pants. Secretly, I hoped she'd never lose that self-assurance.

In the years since, as she approaches her teenage years, her interests have shifted. She loves horses, and on the weekends, we drive her to lessons and shows instead of heading to the trails on foot. I treasured our miles together, and if she decides she wants to run again someday, I'll be happy to pick up where we left off. No matter where her dreams take her, though, I'm here to support her.

I can see that there are moments when the opinions of her classmates get her down or when she doesn't like what she sees in the mirror. I tell her all the time that she's perfect as she is, that she should never change or hide parts of herself to suit someone else's preferences. Sometimes, she even seems to hear me.

But I have to believe that she and Dexter—whose current interests include football and gaming—are both absorbing parts of my story that are more powerful than any words I could say. They watch me sitting in the back of my pickup truck, changing from my foot into my blade, before charging up a hilly trail for 20 miles. They've tracked me for hours and days as I traveled through mountains and across deserts, then walked and run beside me across finish lines. They've seen me on the news and on YouTube and even in a commercial for the Weather Channel, always in shorts and never embarrassed.

I know all this is sinking in because they show me, in their own ways. Eliza's fifth-grade class was assigned to write a report about someone who inspired them. Some of her classmates chose astronauts or famous artists or well-known historical figures. Eliza wrote about me, describing the way I'd fought to get the right equipment, moved from the roads to the trails, and built my own special collection of medals and belt buckles. As for Dexter, I catch him texting his friends about his badass mom running 300 miles, or how cool it is to open the literal book titled *Guinness World Records* and see my name printed inside.

It's plain to them that my disability doesn't define me—that I'm no longer ashamed of who I am but proud of who I've become. I can only hope each of them follows my example and forges their own path. It might be made of dirt or saddle leather or astroturf, but as long as it's truly theirs, it's worth pursuing.

~

While I was wrapping up the final chapters of this book, I turned fifty. Big milestones typically lead to a bit of reflection, and this one was no exception. The night before, I made a list of all I'd done in my forties. I moved from the United Kingdom to the United States. I began my running journey, conquering every distance from 5K to 300 miles. I ran 100 miles on a treadmill and set a world record for consecutive marathons. A couple of years later, I ran 250 half marathons in 250 days.

As I put on my blade to run on the San Tan Trail that morning, I couldn't help but feel excited for my sixth decade and the adventures ahead, some of which were already scheduled. In November, I planned to take on the Great World Race: seven marathons on seven continents in seven consecutive days. Other goals are still there on my bucket list. Someday, I'll return to the Moab 240, for instance. And I dream of tackling the Comrades Marathon, which, despite its name, is an 88-kilometer (54-mile) ultramarathon in South Africa. I grew up watching it on TV, and I've always wanted to test myself on the hilly course.

I also know that not everything will go as planned. Opportunities and obstacles alike will pop up when I least expect them. I'll have to bum-shuffle down the trail at times and, at others, pull my blade out of the sticky mud. Some miles I'll feel great, and others I'll doubt whether I can continue.

When I do, I'll once again look back at how far I've already traveled. I'll remember that all I can do is take the next step forward. And so I do, putting one foot and then one blade in front of the other, up the trail into the mountains.

Afterword

Especially once your story goes national, you never really know who's watching you. During the 104 marathons, and regularly since, I've been amazed by the messages that come in from people all over the world who hear about me and feel inspired.

I often hear from people who have been through similar struggles themselves, or whose loved ones have. Other amputees find my account and realize they too can pursue athletic goals, and they get helpful tips from my posts (and I'm also glad to answer questions or send them resources personally, if they ask me). People newly diagnosed with cancer see what's possible after treatment, and that hope is a powerful force, when you can hang on to it. And sometimes my followers face hard times that have nothing to do with cancer or amputation. Still, they see something in my perseverance that speaks to them, and they write to tell me and thank me.

I take screenshots of all these messages and save them in folders on my phone and on my computer. When I'm having a tough day myself—one where dark clouds hover in my mind, or when a negative comment breaks through the barriers of my confidence—I open them and scroll through, reminding myself of the impact one person can have.

That's how I know that the energy you put out in the world comes back to you, forming a bigger network of support and compassion. In a way, it's like a bigger version of the WhatsApp thread the solo runners relied on during the Speed Project; but this is a worldwide thread of people congratulating each other on their accomplishments and sending extra support to those who are lost or stranded. It's why I continue to post on social media, even though the algorithms often reward anger and rage instead of positivity. I do it because I know every person I reach is worth the effort. And this sentiment is also what compelled me to write this book, even when those bubbles of self-doubt rose to the surface, making me question whether my story was worth telling.

Deep down, I know that it is—and that yours is too.

I hope that you, like Dexter and Eliza, can see the meaning and appreciate the lessons from my journey. Tap into your deeper motivation and let it carry you forward. Chase adventure, whatever that means to you. When you think you can't continue, take one more step up the mountain or across the stream, and then celebrate each tiny bit of progress. Learn to tune out the people who don't value you, stand up to those who don't listen to or appreciate you, and embrace those who join your crew. Never be afraid to cry, to ask for the help you need, to walk instead of run, or to follow the detour that takes you to an even better destination. As you go after those big goals and either reach them or adjust to set new ones, share the journey, with me and with others.

And of course, when you aren't sure how you can keep it all together, try a little duct tape.

Notes

Chapter 1: Find What Drives You

Ewing sarcoma is a rare: Johns Hopkins Medicine. "Ewing Sarcoma in Adults." Accessed September 18, 2025. https://www.hopkinsmedicine.org/health/conditions-and-diseases/sarcoma/ewing-sarcoma-in-adults.

Medical experts still don't: Mayo Clinic. "Ewing Sarcoma: Symptoms and Causes." Accessed September 18, 2025. https://www.mayoclinic.org/diseases-conditions/ewing-sarcoma/symptoms-causes/syc-20351071.

Scientists have found: Hermioni L. Amonoo, Elizabeth Daskalakis, Emma C. Deary, et al. "Gratitude, Optimism, and Satisfaction with Life and Patient-Reported Outcomes in Patients Undergoing Hematopoietic Stem Cell Transplantation." *Psycho-Oncology* 33, no. 2 (2024): e6307. https://doi.org/10.1002/pon.6307.

A literature review also: Klara Knauer, Anne Bach, Norbert Schäffeler, et al. "Personality Traits and Coping Strategies Relevant to Posttraumatic Growth in Patients with Cancer and Survivors: A Systematic Literature Review." *Current Oncology* 29, no. 12 (2022): 9593–9612. https://doi.org/10.3390/curroncol29120754.

In a study of nearly: Liangshan Dong, Shisi Zou, Rong Fan, et al. "The Influence of Athletes' Gratitude on Burnout: The Sequential Mediating Roles of the Coach–Athlete Relationship and Hope." *Frontiers in Psychology* 15 (2024): 1358799. https://doi.org/10.3389/fpsyg.2024.1358799.

And University of Oregon: Christina M. Karns, William E. Moore III, and Ulrich Mayr. "The Cultivation of Pure Altruism via Gratitude: A Functional MRI Study of Change with Gratitude Practice." *Frontiers in Human Neuroscience* 11 (2017): 599. https://doi.org/10.3389/fnhum.2017.00599.

Chapter 5: Celebrate Small Wins

But behavior-change experts: Teresa Amabile and Steven Kramer. *The Progress Principle: Using Small Wins to Ignite Joy, Engagement, and Creativity at Work*. Harvard Business Review Press, 2011.

What's more, it keeps: Melissa Russell. "Why Celebrating Small Wins Matters." Harvard Summer School, May 30, 2024. https://summer.harvard.edu/blog/why-celebrating-small-wins-matters/.

Chapter 6: Rise Above the Haters

Studies show these racing: Wouter Hoogkamer, Shalaya Kipp, Jesse H. Frank, et al. "A Comparison of the Energetic Cost of Running in Marathon Racing Shoes." *Sports Medicine* 48, no. 4 (2018): 1009–19. https://doi.org/10.1007/s40279-017-0811-2; Ashley Mateo. "What Does It Mean to Be a Super Shoe 'Hyper Responder'?" *Run*, October 24, 2023. https://run.outsideonline.com/gear/super-shoe-hyper-responder/.

Rather, the secret sauce: Scott Douglas. "Shoe Prices Are Soaring and Runners Are Suddenly Faster. Welcome to the Age of 'Super Shoes.'" *Runner's World*, June 4, 2025. https://www.runnersworld.com/gear/a64969945/secret-to-super-shoes/.

That's why World Athletics: World Athletics. "Athletic Shoe Regulations: Frequently Asked Questions." PDF document. Accessed September 20, 2025. https://worldathletics.org/download/download?filename=293e972c-8918–48ad-99ef-baac059c1b76.pdf&urlslug=Athletic%20shoe%20regulations%20frequently%20asked%20questions.

Her research showed that: Owen N. Beck, Paolo Taboga, and Alena M. Grabowski. "Sprinting with Prosthetic Versus Biological Legs: Insight from Experimental Data." *Royal Society Open Science* 9, no. 1 (2022): 211799. https://doi.org/10.1098/rsos.211799.

Chapter 8: Be Your Own Advocate

Given that the median: Jordan Smith. "Follow This Expert-Approved Advice on Creating an Annual Running Plan." *Runner's World,* January 15, 2025. https://www.runnersworld.com/training/a63424582/annual-running-plan/.

Chapter 9: Don't Be Afraid to Cry

Research shows that secondary: Shi-Kai Wang, Min Feng, Yu Fang, et al. "Psychological Trauma, Posttraumatic Stress Disorder and Trauma-Related Depression: A Mini-Review." *World Journal of Psychiatry* 13, no. 6 (2023): 331–39. https://doi.org/10.5498/wjp.v13.i6.331.

Chapter 11: Build a Team

As the former *Runner's World*: Bill Katovsky. *1,001 Pearls of Runners' Wisdom: Advice and Inspiration for the Open Road.* Skyhorse Publishing, 2012.

Sometimes, even more than: Chris Hartley and Pete Coffee. "Perceived and Received Dimensional Support: Main and Stress-Buffering Effects on Dimensions of Burnout." *Frontiers in Psychology* 10 (2019): 1724. https://doi.org/10.3389/fpsyg.2019.01724.

Chapter 13: Set Big Goals, Then Adapt to Achieve

But as famed martial artist: Quote attributed to Bruce Lee. "A goal is not always meant to be reached, it often serves simply as something to aim at." Bruce Lee X (Twitter) account (@brucelee), September 15, 2020. https://x.com/brucelee/status/1305778432173838336.

There's a sentiment I like: Quote attributed to Winston S. Churchill. Accessed September 20, 2025. https://www.goodreads.com/quotes/3270-success-is-not-final-failure-is-not-fatal-it-is.

In a commencement speech: Dartmouth College website. "2024 Commencement Address by Roger Federer." June 9, 2024. https://home.dartmouth.edu/news/2024/06/2024-commencement-address-roger-federer.

Reading Group Guide

1. Have you ever run a marathon or thought about doing so? Why or why not?

2. Did you know about the different athletic tools/blades available to amputees? What do you think of the expense of such tools?

3. What are you grateful for in life? What do you think are the best ways to show gratitude? Do you believe that acknowledging what you're grateful for can make you a happier person?

4. Where do you prefer to exercise? Do you like to go out in nature, stroll through the city, hit the gym, or stay at home?

5. What kinds of criticism and prejudice did Jacky face because of her leg? Why is it important to educate yourself about people with different experiences than yours? What prejudices or biases might arise without such education?

6. Were you raised to show your emotions or to suppress them? How do you feel about showing your emotions now? Is it difficult for you to be open about how you're feeling? Do you think it's important to do so?

7. Jacky stresses the need for a team during her longer runs and marathons. Can you think of a time in your life or work where you needed the support of a team to get through? How was that support helpful to you?

8. Discuss times when you grew from failure or a mistake. What helped you grow from there? Then, consider a time when you grew from success. How was that growth similar or different to the growth from failure?

9. Do you have large goals you've set for yourself in life? How are you attempting to reach those goals? Have you thought about what your next goals might be after achieving the first?

10. Jacky hopes to be a good role model for everyone but especially for her children. Is being a good role model important to you? What do you think makes someone a good role model?

11. What do you think of Jacky's accomplishment of running 104 marathons in 104 consecutive days? Can you imagine the effort it would take to do something like that?

Acknowledgments

From Jacky

Writing a book is its own kind of ultramarathon—one that takes years! I'm grateful for all the support and encouragement I received from my team along the way.

First and foremost, thank you to my family—my husband and kiddos. Edwin, you're my true partner in running and everything else, and I can't imagine this adventure without you. Dexter and Eliza, you give my life purpose and meaning. I'm so glad to be your mum, and I can't wait to see where your own paths take you.

Thank you to my brother, Lionel. You stepped up when I didn't even know I needed you, and I'll forever appreciate it. Whoever thought sleeping in the back of a truck could be so restful?

To Stephany Evans, my agent, thank you for believing in my story from the beginning. And thank you to the team at Sourcebooks, especially senior editorial director Anna Michels. Anna, I knew from the moment I saw the medals on your wall that you were the right person to bring this book to life. I'm also grateful to designer Emily Mahar for the beautiful cover; production editor Mary Wheelehan and copy editor Lisa K. Marietta for their thoughtful comments and attention to detail; and Angela Corpus, Gianna Antolos, and Daisy Rankin on the marketing team. And of course, thank you to my coauthor, Cindy Kuzma, who helped me put my feelings and experiences into sentences and chapters. I couldn't have done this without you.

To all those who have shared miles with me and supported my off-the-wall ideas, thank you. This includes but isn't limited to Jeannette Pantani, Rachel Zelibor, Rachel Belmont, Tara and Tony Gerlach, Mike and Alisa Zoccoli, Katie Williams, Michael Dwomoh (Dr. D), Josh Underwood, Jennifer and Dave Goins, Mike Barclay, Mirna Valerio, and Meb Keflezighi. I'm grateful too to the many race directors and officials who have made me feel welcome, including Joe Randene, Trent Swanson, and many more. Thank you as well to the doctors, prosthetists, and other healthcare providers who treated my cancer and helped me thrive afterward.

I'd also like to thank my sponsors—Altra, Garmin, NOW Foods, Ultimate Direction, Squirrel's Nut Butter, and Fillauer—and the other companies who have supported my efforts, including RXBAR. And I so appreciate the work of organizations like Amputee Blade Runners, the Move for Jenn Foundation, Team Catapult, and the Challenged Athletes Foundation in helping para-athletes connect to the equipment they need.

Finally, I'm grateful to every supporter who's followed my journey on social media or elsewhere—and especially those who have shared their own stories with me. You've given me strength and motivation when I needed it the most; my greatest hope is that, through this book, I can return the favor.

From Cindy

Thank you so much, Jacky, for inviting me to join your crew—it's been an honor! I'm beyond grateful to agent Stephany Evans; Anna Michels and the whole fantastic team at Sourcebooks; and all the colleagues and editors who have informed and strengthened my storytelling over the years, including Sarah Lorge Butler, who edited my story about Jacky for *Runner's World*. Thanks also to my parents, Bill and Mary Szelag, for believing in me, and my equally amazing and supportive in-laws, Matt, Lucas, and Charlene Kuzma (Char, I miss you, so much). And to my Matt, for all the things, always.

About the Authors

Jacky Hunt-Broersma is an amputee ultrarunner based in Arizona, a motivational speaker, mom, coach, and cancer survivor who aims to inspire people worldwide by redefining what's possible. After losing her leg to Ewing sarcoma, she turned to running—pushing past limits and shattering stereotypes about disability and endurance.

In 2022, she made history by running 104 marathons in 104 consecutive days, setting a Guinness World Record. She also ran 300 miles from Los Angeles to Las Vegas through the grueling Mojave Desert, proving that barriers are meant to be broken.

Beyond the miles, she is a dedicated mom, an advocate for adaptive athletes, and a storyteller who uses her journey to remind everyone: You're stronger than you think.

Cindy Kuzma is a Chicago-based journalist who specializes in endurance sports, fitness, and health. She's the coauthor of *Rebound: Train Your Mind to Bounce Back Stronger from Sports Injuries* (Bloomsbury Sport, 2019, with Carrie Jackson Cheadle) and *Breakthrough Women's*

Running: Dream Big and Train Smart (Human Kinetics, 2022, with Neely Spence Gracey). She earned her master's degree from Northwestern University's Medill School of Journalism and has spent the past twenty-plus years writing for national print and online publications, including *Runner's World*, the *New York Times*, *Women's Running*, *SELF*, and *Front Office Sports*. She is also the cohost of the *Injured Athletes Club* podcast and on the leadership committee for Starting Line 1928, an oral history project preserving the voices of women's running pioneers.